trust us...
they'll ask

ANSWERS to your kids' toughest
and most awkward QUESTIONS

Loveland, Colorado
group.com

Group resources actually work!

This Group resource incorporates our R.E.A.L. approach to ministry. It reinforces a growing friendship with Jesus, encourages long-term learning, and results in life transformation, because it's

Relational
Learner-to-learner interaction enhances learning and builds Christian friendships.

Experiential
What learners experience through discussion and action sticks with them up to 9 times longer than what they simply hear or read.

Applicable
The aim of Christian education is to equip learners to be both hearers and doers of God's Word.

Learner-based
Learners understand and retain more when the learning process takes into consideration how they learn best.

Trust Us...They'll Ask
Copyright © 2011 Group Publishing, Inc.
Visit our website: **group.com**

Unless otherwise indicated, all Scripture quotations are taken from the *Holy Bible,* New Living Translation, copyright © 1996, 2004, 2007. Used by permission of Tyndale House Publishers, Inc., Carol Stream, Illinois 60188. All rights reserved.

Credits
Authors: Bill Anderson, Nick Diliberto, Gloria Lee, Anthony Meyers, Ricardo Miller, Gigi Schweikert, and Johnny Scott
Editor: Mikal Keefer
Cover Design: RoseAnne Sather
Interior Design: Suzi Jensen

ISBN 978-0-7644-4911-6
10 9 8 7 6 5 4 3 2 1   16 15 14 13 12 11
Printed in the United States of America.

Foreword

Ah, those awkward parenting moments...

Sheila was zipping through the grocery checkout line with her first-grader when hers arrived. As the cashier scanned a head of lettuce, Sheila heard a familiar little voice ask: "Mommy, what is oral sex?"

A memorable moment for all in earshot—and the reason Sheila changed grocery stores for six months. She wasn't sure she could ever face that cashier again!

We want our kids to talk with us. To ask us—rather than their friends—the hard questions about life. About sex and God. About right and wrong.

Except we're terrified that when they do, we'll drop the ball. We won't know what to say...and our children will walk away unsatisfied.

And thinking we're idiots.

Relax—here's help!

Sooner or later your child will ask most of the 100+ questions you'll find in this helpful book. It may be at the grocery store, while you're riding in the car, or in the middle of a church service, but you can be sure these questions are coming.

And now you'll be ready with an age-appropriate answer...and relevant Bible references to help you and your child explore God's perspective on the issue at hand.

We assembled a crack team of child and preteen experts and parents to help you prepare for your awkward moments. They've crafted answers that will satisfy your children and open up ongoing communication.

So relax—you're not alone.

And your kids will think you're brilliant!

We'll help you launch the conversation.

You don't have to wait until your child asks about a topic, you know.

Use this book to raise issues in a natural way. You'll equip your child to handle sensitive topics when they arise at school or on the playground. And you'll help cement a Christian worldview in place that blesses your child all through life.

Plus, when you pick the moment, you're assured of your child's undivided attention and the time for a relaxed conversation.

Oh—and enjoy the awkward moments...

They're part of the joy of parenting.

And they make wonderful stories to share with your kids later!

> The information in this book is meant to be a guide for you to handle questions posed by your children. This is not professional advice meant to replace what you'd receive from licensed counselors or psychologists.

The Authors

Bill Anderson

Bill Anderson is a veteran children's and family life pastor. He's a regular contributor to Children's Ministry Magazine and Children's Ministry Professional Edition.

Nick Diliberto

Nick Diliberto is a noted preteen ministry expert, the creator of PreteenMinistry.net, and a children's director in San Diego.

Gloria Lee

Gloria Lee is a veteran children's minister who speaks on ministry issues at workshops and conventions across the U.S. She resides in California.

(continued)

Anthony Meyers

Anthony Meyers is a former children's and youth pastor. He's also a motivational speaker, a professor, and a pastor (anthonymeyers .com).

Ricardo Miller

Ricardo Miller is a veteran children's minister, a sought-after speaker, and the founder of Ricardo Miller Children's Ministries (ricardo miller.com).

Gigi Schweikert

Gigi Schweikert (gigischweikert.com) is the author of seven books and numerous articles. She formerly directed the United Nations Early Childhood Program in New York.

Johnny Scott

Johnny Scott is a preteen expert. He's the program director of Christ In Youth's Believe Tour. When not on the road at a Believe conference, he's playing with the worship band Foundation Red.

Table of
Contents

Sexuality

Grown-ups & Kids

Boy Stuff & Girl Stuff

Good & Bad, Right & Wrong

Family & Friends

Fears

God

Church & Angels, Heaven & Hell

Imponderables

Sexuality

Q: What is sex?

Preschooler:
Your preschooler doesn't need to know—and won't understand. He *will* grasp "God made boys and girls differently." That explanation will satisfy a younger preschooler; an older one might press for more details. If so, explain simply that boys have penises and girls don't.

Elementary-Age:
At this age your child needs to understand the basics, reproductive organs included. Why? Because if you don't share, others will. *How* you share information is as important—don't be embarrassed. Review basic biology so you're comfortable using correct terms. Discuss what's coming in puberty. Invite questions and ongoing dialogue. And casually check: Why is the question being raised at this time?

Preteen:
Include not just the "how" of sex but also the "why." Stress that sex is a *good* thing, one God expects to be enjoyed in the context of marriage between a husband and wife. Explain the bonding that sexual relations brings—and the pain of breakups if sex has been involved. Thank your child for asking, and offer to be a resource in your child's life.

Related Scriptures: For preschoolers, Genesis 2:7, 19-24 is appropriate. For elementary and preteen kids, let Ephesians 5:31 inform your discussions.

How can Aunt Susie have a baby if she isn't married?

Preschooler:
Tell your preschooler that all babies are made by God and that God wants babies to have mommies and daddies who love them. God prefers that Aunt Susie be married so she and her baby can have a husband and daddy to love and care for them.

Elementary-Age:
Most elementary children see sex and marriage as the same thing. If they don't understand sex and conception, they'll believe you must be married to conceive. This is a good time to have the "sex talk." (See page 12 for help!) Sex was created by God as a good and enjoyable way for married people to express their love and have children. Sometimes people have sex when they aren't married, and that's not God's plan.

Preteen:
Having sex outside of marriage can result in having a baby, and that's not best for either the baby or the unmarried couple. Talk to your child about abstinence until marriage, assuring your child that sex is "worth waiting for." Tell your children their bodies are treasures to be given away only to their husbands or wives.

Related Scriptures: First Corinthians 7:2 describes God's plan for sex within marriage.

How does a baby come out of a mommy's stomach?

Preschooler:

Preschoolers are often satisfied with simple answers, so don't panic or go into great detail. Explain that doctors help the baby out. If your preschooler probes further, explain that God made mommy's body so that babies can come out of a special place. Only answer what she asks, and don't lie.

Elementary-Age:

This may feel awkward—but if you don't make it a big deal, your child won't either. Simply give the facts. Keep it simple, and let your child set the pace. Don't be scared to use words like *C-section* or *vagina*. Do an online search of reliable medical websites—together—for more information if your child wants it.

Preteen:

Your preteen is old enough to know the specifics. Preteens may have more detailed questions, but don't shy away. Be honest, and use the correct terminology. Talk about conception, prenatal development, and the process of labor. This may open up even more questions, but no matter how weird it feels, appropriately answer them.

Related Scriptures: Genesis 3:16 is a good resource for older children. This passage traces pain in childbirth back to original sin, so it could lead to a very teachable moment!

Q: **Why do mommies and daddies get to sleep in the same bed, but I can't sleep in the same bed with my friends that are boys/girls?**

Preschooler:

Most preschoolers won't see this as an issue. Every family has its own sleeping habits, and some preschoolers sleep with siblings of the opposite gender. If your child asks, it's likely an innocent question. Simply state boys and girls usually sleep in separate beds until they're married.

Elementary-Age:

Elementary kids already know boys and girls are physically different. Let them know that as their bodies change during puberty, they should become more private with their bodies—such as using gender-specific restrooms and dressing modestly. Part of keeping our bodies private includes not sleeping in the same bed unless you're married.

Preteen:

This answer gets complicated if your preteen knows unwed couples or has been inquisitive about what she's seen on TV and in movies. Honestly discuss your family values, acknowledging they may be very different from others' values. Let her know that being careful with her body is an important part of honoring God—even if her sleepover friend's just a friend!

Related Scriptures: See 1 Corinthians 6:19-20, and let Genesis 39:1-20 and Romans 12:2 guide your discussion with preteens.

Q: What's a condom?

Preschooler:

Preschoolers won't understand but will still want a simple answer. Tell your preschooler that adults use condoms. Also, find out where she might have seen or heard about a condom.

Elementary-Age:

If you haven't had the sex talk with your child yet, this may be the time. Yes, it's awkward, but better to hear correct information from you. Explain why people use condoms. Embrace curiosity. Answer honestly. Keep it simple, letting your child know that a condom is like a raincoat to cover a penis. This should satisfy your child's curiosity. If not, provide additional information as is consistent with your family's values.

Preteen:

Explain "safe sex" and that a condom is used as a contraception to avoid pregnancy, as well as a way to stay safe from sexually transmitted diseases. There's debate over the distribution of condoms in middle and high schools; ask your preteen what she thinks. Reiterate to your preteen that God designed sex to be shared between a husband and wife. The Bible teaches abstinence in all other situations. In a quiet, open way, share your expectations about sexual behavior with your preteen.

Related Scriptures: See 1 Corinthians 7:2 and Ephesians 5:3. Hebrews 13:4 can guide your conversation with preteens.

Why do you have hair down there?

Preschooler:
Preschoolers are very observant—when yours starts to ask questions like this, it's best to start practicing more modesty around the house. Explain that people's bodies change as they get older. Tell your preschooler she will grow taller and grow hair in new places, too.

Elementary-Age:
Prepare your child for the changes his or her body will undergo in the next few years: genital, leg, and underarm hair; body odor; menstruation for girls; and erections for boys. Your daughter is likely to try shaving on her own with painful results if you don't provide coaching, so educate her and demonstrate how to shave. Try not to make a big deal about bodily changes; children this age embarrass easily.

Preteen:
Educate your preteen about genital hygiene. Yes, like it or not, that's a parental job. For girls, decide if shaving or hair removal around the bikini line needs to be addressed. Talk to your daughter about modesty and appropriate clothing. For boys, educate about protecting and cleaning the genital area, especially if they're involved in sports.

Related Scriptures: God expects us to take care of our bodies. See Romans 12:1 and 1 Corinthians 6:19-20.

Q: What is oral sex?

Preschooler:
It's unlikely preschoolers will ask this unless they've heard the term from older children. Although they won't understand oral sex or sex, this is a great opportunity to say that sex is one way God planned for a mommy and daddy to show their love for each other. Don't be afraid to use the word *sex* or call genitals by the proper terms, *vagina* and *penis*.

Elementary-Age:
Unfortunately, your elementary child is likely to hear this term and it's best to address it yourself. You can describe oral sex as a married couple kissing each other's private parts or genitals. Eye-opening yes, but that's what it is. Discuss this within the context of God's design for marital sex and conception.

Preteen:
Oral sex is common among many high-schoolers and some middle-schoolers—including Christian youth. Most don't consider it "real" sex since you can't get pregnant. Many also believe oral sex does not compromise abstinence. Explain that all sexual acts, not just intercourse, should occur only within the boundaries of marriage.

Related Scriptures: Ephesians 5:31 speaks of man and woman becoming one in marriage. First Corinthians 7:2-5 discusses sexual activity in marriage.

Do gay people choose to be gay, or are they born that way?

Preschooler:
Be sure your preschooler knows what *gay* means in this context. Explain that *gay* describes a man who wants to marry another man, or a woman who wants to marry another woman. If your child asks, share that the Bible says God made men and women to marry each other. Remind your child everyone sins, but God forgives and loves everyone.

Elementary-Age:
Explain to your child that this is a much-debated topic. Admit we don't know why some people are born more likely to have homosexual behavior, but some are. The Bible says homosexual activities are sin just like any other sin, but God loves sinners even though he dislikes sin. And God can forgive all sins. Since God shows love to everyone, that's what he wants us to do, too.

Preteen:
Homosexuality is a sensitive subject, even among Christians. If you have a conviction on this issue, share it your child. We know the Bible indicates that everyone sins, and homosexual activity is just one of those sins. Explain homosexuality is not a "greater" sin than others. God loves everyone the same, and all sins are forgivable. Tell your preteen we need to treat everyone with love and respect, and not judge them based on sexual preference.

Related Scriptures: See Romans 1:24-27 and 1 Corinthians 6:9-11 about homosexuality, and Ephesians 1:7 and James 1:13-15 about temptation and forgiveness.

How come there are dirty pictures of girls on the Internet?

Preschooler:
Unfortunately, even preschoolers can stumble onto inappropriate websites. Set parental controls on your computers and TVs, and never let preschoolers be online alone. If your preschooler does find pictures, explain that since God made the human body, we should look at it in ways that make God happy. God doesn't want us to look at pictures of people without clothes on. Explore how your preschooler has been exposed to questionable pictures.

Elementary-Age:
Set computer guidelines and review them with your child. Talk about inappropriate websites that you don't want your child to visit, including sites with pictures of naked people. Explain that there are people who like looking at these pictures, but that God wants us to think about and look at good things and to respect others. Looking at pictures of people without their clothes on doesn't show respect.

Preteen:
There are many people who engage in inappropriate activities, including pornography. Explain that some people use pornography to make money, but it hurts people. Talk to your preteens about why people like looking at these pictures online. Not everything that makes us curious or feel good is good for us. Discuss the why and how of resisting temptation and living a life pleasing to God.

Related Scriptures: Philippians 4:8 speaks to the need to avoid what compromises us; Matthew 5:28 the seriousness of lust.

Q: Will I go to hell for masturbating?

Preschooler:
Preschoolers (hopefully) haven't yet learned about masturbation, but they know their bodies give them pleasure. Talk with them about the need to respect their bodies by touching appropriately, which means they don't touch their genitals unless they're washing or going to the bathroom. Also mention that no one else should touch them anywhere a bathing suit would cover, except the doctor during a doctor's appointment.

Elementary-Age:
Masturbation isn't specifically addressed in the Bible—but thinking about the opposite sex in a way that will elicit lust (a desire to see them naked) is mentioned…as a sin. The sexual fantasies that normally accompany masturbation are more problematic than the simple sexual act, as they impact how we view and objectify others. However, God can forgive us for any sin, so we won't go to hell if we've had sexual fantasies.

Preteen:
It's the rare preteen who isn't tempted to masturbate. As uncomfortable as that thought is for parents, it's true…and if your preteen raises a concern, address it without passing judgment. It's not okay to objectify the opposite sex (or a particular person) in such a way as to use them for your own personal, sexual pleasure. Masturbation encourages lust, or thinking about other people sexually—which is a sin. Like all sins, lust is forgivable and your child won't be condemned to hell for it. But lust grows ever more entrenched as your preteen continues to view members of the opposite sex as objects rather than people.

Related Scriptures: Matthew 5:28-29 and 1 Thessalonians 4:1-8 address lust.

Q: If I'm a boy and I like another boy, does that mean I'm gay?

Preschooler:

Explain that boys can be best friends with other boys, and girls with other girls. Having friends doesn't mean you're "gay"; it means you have friends. Your preschooler won't understand homosexuality, so table that topic for later.

Elementary-Age:

No—even having a "crush" on another child of the same sex doesn't mean someone is gay. But it raises a question: Is your child struggling with feelings for the same sex? If so, discuss it calmly and seek the services of a capable therapist with experience helping children sort out their sexual orientation. While expressing support and acceptance, also share the Bible's perspective about being gay.

Preteen:

Explore your preteen's thoughts about homosexuality, and seek to discover what's prompting the question. Is it simple curiosity—or something more? This is likely uncharted water for you; do your best to keep the lines of communication open in discussing this topic. No gay-bashing. Be transparent about your own feelings, but be mindful they're not the highest priority. If your preteen thinks he might be gay, seek qualified help in exploring his gender issues.

Related Scriptures: Romans 1:27 reflects the seriousness of homosexuality; Matthew 7:1-5 the seriousness of judging others.

Q: **Did you have sex before you were married?**

Preschooler:
It's unlikely your preschooler will ask about this. If it comes up, explain that God has given husbands and wives the chance to love each other in special ways. We obey God when we wait until we're married to enjoy that special way. But we can obey God in lots of ways right now—by caring about people and doing as God asks.

Elementary-Age:
You may decide to tell your child that's a personal question that you don't want to answer at the moment. But it's powerful when kids learn from our mistakes. If you had sex before marriage and choose to tell your child that, be clear that by sharing your story, you're not giving your child permission. You're admitting to a painful mistake that's had consequences. Be careful about saying much; don't give details. If your child is a result of premarital sex, emphasize that your child is a blessing God gave you even though you didn't obey him. But even though God can do good things in response to our sins, he wants us to obey him.

Preteen:
Share your personal story honestly—not to give permission but to warn of the consequences of making a mistake. Be clear: Obeying God's plan and timing in our lives brings blessing. Disobeying God often brings pain. If your child was conceived out of wedlock, mention that God is loving and can bring good out of our wrong choices—and your child is one of those good things. But God wants us to obey him and trust his plan.

Related Scriptures: Principles to remember as you decide what you'll share: Ephesians 4:29; Colossians 3:9-10; and 1 Thessalonians 5:11.

Grown-ups
& Kids

Why is it okay for parents to spank kids when kids can't hit anyone?

Preschooler:

Whether you do or don't employ corporal punishment in your family, it's important you and your child understand parents never enjoy spanking and don't do it in anger. Spanking is punishment—controlled and delivered to help kids know not to do things that could hurt them. When kids hit each other, the intention is usually to be mean, to hurt, or to retaliate. Hitting is rooted in anger; spanking is rooted in love. If you do spank your child, calmly explain why you're doing it in the moment.

Elementary-Age:

Like it or not, it's God's idea that parents who love their children discipline and shape them. That's true whether a family employs spanking or not. Explore your child's feelings about discipline in general. If you've spanked in the past, your child might well be ready for you to remove that discipline tool from your parental tool chest.

Preteen:

Discuss what motivates parents to spank children—and if you've had experience spanking or being spanked, share your story. Admit that there are parents who lash out at their children in anger, sometimes physically. That isn't discipline; it's abuse—and needs to be treated as such.

Related Scriptures: Proverbs 3:12; 6:20; and Ephesians 6:4 talk about the goals of discipline. Proverbs 13:24; 23:13-14; and 29:15 speak to corporal punishment.

Why do adults get to do whatever they want?

Preschooler:

To preschoolers, who are told what to do about almost everything, it certainly appears as though adults have it made. We stay up as late as we wish and eat what we want, when we want. Explain that adults and children must both listen to God and obey his rules. And God told parents to raise their children.

Elementary-Age:

This question usually pops up when a child doesn't get what she wants. Elementary-age children desire more independence and think parents have it easy (if only they knew!). Validate that adults *do* have more choices, but we still have to follow rules—the laws, but most importantly, what God says. Allow your child to make more choices when possible. Practicing making choices now leads to making better choices later.

Preteen:

Tell your preteen she's right—adults get to do what they want. But every choice comes with a consequence. When we follow God's plan for us and let the Bible guide us, we're more likely to make good choices. As your preteen demonstrates responsibility, give her more opportunities to make choices.

Related Scriptures: Matthew 5:14-16 speaks of how we represent Christ through the choices we make. Micah 6:8 tells how to live.

Do pastors and Sunday school teachers do bad stuff, too?

Preschooler:
In a word: yes. Even people who help us learn about God make mistakes and do things that make God sad. Share with your preschooler that God is always willing to forgive us and help us do better.

Elementary-Age:
Your elementary-age child has probably heard about sin entering the world through Adam and Eve, but may not have connected the dots all the way to herself—and the Christian leaders in her life. Assure her that while people may disappoint us, God never will. Encourage your child to be forgiving and have grace for those who stumble—just as God has grace for her.

Preteen:
Remind your preteen that having a leadership role is no guarantee of perfection. Even the Apostle Paul considered himself "chief among sinners." If this question arose from a sense of personal failure, reassure your child of God's forgiveness and the Holy Spirit's intent to give her power to live a faithful life. If criticism is fueling the question, pray together for your fallen leaders. Model grace.

Related Scriptures: We all sin: See Romans 3:23 and 1 Timothy 1:15.

How come you can watch movies I can't watch?

Preschooler:
Explain that God expects parents to guard and protect their children's eyes and ears from things children shouldn't see until they are old enough to see them.

Elementary-Age:
Explain that our media choices impact our behavior; studies have proven it. Your child may be responding to a double standard: Why is an "R" movie okay for you and not him? Actually, that's a good question. Explain that the older you get, the more you understand whether or not you can handle the violence and sexual content in films. Even adults need to avoid movies that will make them think about or do bad things. Trust us: That's an answer that won't satisfy. Better: Consider limiting *your* movie picks, too—to honor your child.

Preteen:
Correct the misperception: As children grow older, they don't "get to" watch bad things. Nor should adults. The goal isn't to push the furthest edge of entertainment to allow as much as possible, but to in all things honor God. Dig into the verses below to help your preteen understand what it means to honor God. Discuss how you and your preteen— together—can apply that truth to your entertainment choices.

Related Scriptures: Matthew 18:5-7; 1 Corinthians 10:23; and Philippians 4:7-9 speak to our decisions and the consequences.

Q: Why didn't my birth mom want me?

Preschooler:

Preschoolers can't process all the details of their birth circumstances. Hug often and be sure your preschooler is secure in knowing he's loved and wanted by you—and God!

Elementary-Age:

Your elementary child may not be ready for all the details. Explain his birth mom couldn't take care of him, so to show her love for her precious baby, she gave her baby to someone who could provide care—and who deeply wanted him. Stress that he's loved and wanted, and God has great plans for him.

Preteen:

It's vital your preteen be secure in knowing God created and loves him and you love and want him. You may be able to give him more details about why his birth mom couldn't take care of him at the time. Stress that you're blessed and thankful to be the one who gets to take care of him now. Hug time!

Related Scriptures: Share stories of Moses (Exodus 1–2) and Esther—both were adopted and used by God in mighty ways. Read Psalm 27:10 to emphasize God's love even when we feel abandoned. For preteens who've been adopted, Ephesians 1:5 may help them understand that all Christians are adopted into God's family. Adoption is a wonderful thing!

Q: Why am I ugly?

Preschooler:

Help your preschooler discover God made him just the way he is—which is wonderful!—on purpose. Your complete acceptance and affirmation, communicated through word and deed, will go a long way toward instilling confidence and a positive self-image.

Elementary-Age:

Help kids focus on who they *are* rather than how they look. Teach them to value character in themselves (and others) over outward appearances, and to do as God does: Look at the heart. Help them know that true beauty is on the inside. The foundation you're building now must support your child through his preteen and teen years.

Preteen:

Your child is being pressured to always look good, even as his body goes through intense physical, emotional, and social changes. Consistently affirm your child's value as a person—not a pinup—and help your preteen look to God for affirmation, rather than the mirror. That said, do help your child with basic fashion and hygiene; most bad hair days can easily be avoided.

Related Scriptures: Read 1 Samuel 16:7 and Psalm 139:13-14 with your child for God's take on lookin' good.

Q: Who do you love more: me or Daddy?

Preschooler:
Your preschooler often needs reassurance that you love her. Explain that you love her and Daddy both very much—and that Daddy loves her, too.

Elementary-Age:
Your elementary-age child is old enough to realize that you love people in different ways. Share that you love your child one way, your spouse another, a friend differently still. Tell your child that there's enough room in your heart for everyone you love, and that you'll never run out of love for your child. Reassure your child you love her with all your heart—and toss in a hug for good measure!

Preteen:
Share that comparing love is like comparing clothes; there are different kinds for different seasons. God loves us all equally, and God has given us appropriate ways to love each other equally. Reassure your child that even if there's more conflict in the home than usual (it often arrives with the preteen years), you love her completely, wildly, desperately, and in a different way than you love Daddy. If she'll accept it, give her a long, heartfelt hug.

Related Scriptures: God reminds us of his love in Jeremiah 31:3, and to love others in John 15:12.

Does God love Mom even if she doesn't come to church?

Preschooler:

Yes, God loves everyone. Preschoolers may view going to church as proof we love God, and that's not necessarily the case. Assure your preschooler that while God would welcome Mom in church, God won't stop loving her if she doesn't go.

Elementary-Age:

If your child has been taught church attendance is a good thing (and it is), there will be a conflict if Mom doesn't go. He may begin to question why Mom doesn't go, and this may lead to some interesting conversations. Encourage your child to attend church and now and then to invite Mom to go along. Let him know God loves Mom, and that he can show God's love to Mom with kindness and respect.

Preteen:

If Mom isn't going because she's not a Christian, encourage your child to honor Mom and show her God's love by obeying God and Mom out of love. If Mom has been hurt by the church, suggest that together you ask Mom to consider working through that offense. Bottom line: Your child can be a positive or negative influence in this situation. Brainstorm with your preteen what "positive" might look like, and prayerfully give the situation to God.

Related Scriptures: Ephesians 6:2 is a reminder to honor parents, and Hebrews 10:25 encourages church attendance.

Boy Stuff &
Girl Stuff

What if I have a crush on someone? What do I do?

Preschooler:
Your preschooler may have special friends and often the selection process is gender neutral. Avoid identifying an other-gender child as "your little girlfriend" or "your first boyfriend" and your child won't feel odd about it.

Elementary-Age:
First crushes come with the territory. Encourage your child to get to know someone he likes. Suggest your child spend time with his "crush" in a group setting and discover what it is about the person that's likable. Let your child know you're available to talk about crushes, but don't prod. Respect your child's privacy and don't try to force your child to open up.

Preteen:
Crushes—and crushed hearts—are par for this part of your child's development. The first is natural, and you can help soften the latter by encouraging your child to have a realistic view of the person. Suggest your child get to know her: what she likes and dislikes, and what he finds attractive about her. The social skills and perspective gained now will serve your child for a lifetime. And don't tease your child—that will slam shut the doors of communication.

Related Scriptures: Don't let a crush consume you, and remember that strong faith is what really makes a person attractive—see 2 Corinthians 6:14-15 and 2 Timothy 2:22. God is willing to help us deal with crushes: See James 1:5.

Q: Can boys wear pink, too?

Preschooler:
Girls don't "own" pink. Blue and pink send signals when children are infants to tip off observers as to a child's sex, but by preschool children can embrace a wide range of colors. If your male child balks at wearing pink, it may be because of ridicule; allow your preschooler to choose his favorite colors.

Elementary-Age:
Fashion choices—including colors—are often set by peers during the elementary-age years. Save yourself ongoing battles and let your child help make clothing purchase choices—at least as far as colors are concerned. If your son wants to wear pink, let him! But if it's embarrassing, let him pick colors he prefers.

Preteen:
Expressing oneself through clothing can be fun. It can also lead to public ridicule, untrue perceptions, and lonely lunches. Discuss with your child what associations are often made with pink—that girls typically wear pink. Claim this as a teachable moment concerning stereotypes, and note that many non-gay men wear pink. Once your child has the information, support his decision about pink—no matter what he decides.

Related Scriptures: Deuteronomy 22:5 addresses cross-dressing, and 1 Corinthians 6:19-20 our need to glorify God in all our choices.

How come God made girls without a penis?

Preschooler:

Ah—the age-old question of "who has one and who doesn't." Preschoolers are fascinated by their bodies, especially as they toilet train. Explain that God made boys and girls differently: Boys have a penis and girls have a vagina. The vagina is on the inside so girls can have a baby when they are married. And use correct terminology from the start.

Elementary-Age:

Explain that God made boys and girls exactly as he wanted them: Boys have a penis while girls have a vagina, which is inside their bodies. Boys and girls are designed so they can fit together to create babies when they're older and married. This is a good time to talk about modesty. Remind children that anything a bathing suit would cover is something they should keep private.

Preteen:

If your child isn't already aware, explain that God made the penis to fit inside the vagina when a man and woman get married. Also bear in mind that children's bodies begin changing during the preteen years. Review the basic biology—proper terms, especially—before changes begin. Too late? Then explain good hygiene, including that related to genitals. Girls should understand menstruation, and boys should know about erections and the causes for them. Help preteens feel comfortable about their changing bodies.

Related Scriptures: Psalm 139:14 reassures us that we are made just as God intended. Romans 12:1 teaches that we should keep our bodies holy.

Q: Who's better—boys or girls?

Preschooler:

Expect your preschooler to believe some activities are for girls and some for boys. But the real answer to this question is "neither"—sometimes a boy is better at something…sometimes a girl is better at it. Encourage your child to not to make life a boy/girl competition; there's room for us all to be successes.

Elementary-Age:

Your child sees how gender roles play out at school, home, and church. Share your view of what the Bible says about gender roles but stress one isn't "better" than the other. It's okay to be a girl who can spike a volleyball or a boy who knits sweaters. Society places a "good, better, best" value on people; both boys *and* girls are beloved children of God…and that's the highest value in the universe.

Preteen:

Preteens are *acutely* aware of gender differences. Shouts of "cooties" are quickly being replaced by nods toward the "cuties." Validate your child's emerging sexual identity; let your child know you're proud of her. And especially if you have sons *and* daughters, don't be suckered into answering this question!

Related Scriptures: First Corinthians 11:3 and 1 Timothy 2:11-12 speak to gender differences; Galatians 3:26-28 to our equality in Christ.

The kids are calling me a name—what is a virgin?

Preschooler:

The teasing may well be a bigger issue than being called a virgin. Explain *virgin* isn't a bad word, but teasing is never okay. Talk about what your preschooler should do the next time he's teased. Encourage your child to respond to teasing with kindness and to remember that God made him just the way he is.

Elementary-Age:

If you've already talked about sex with your child, simply define *virgin* as someone who's never had sex. Reassure him it's not a bad word—but the teasing may be painful. Focus on your child's feelings, and encourage him to forgive and stand up for himself when kids tease him. Pray with your child for comfort, healing, courage, and a heart of forgiveness.

Preteen:

It's okay to explain what *virgin* means—someone who's never had sex. And encourage your child that *virgin* is a good name, because God wants us to wait until we're married to have sex. The bigger issue is probably the teasing and bullying. Comfort your preteen, and share how Jesus was teased and understands our hurts. The natural reaction is to hurt others in return, but God wants us to forgive and love our enemies. Pray together and devise an action plan to deal with being teased.

Related Scriptures: David dealt with teasing in 1 Samuel 17—share with younger children. For dealing with bullies, refer to Luke 6:27-28; Ephesians 4:31-32; and 1 Peter 3:9.

When can I have a boyfriend/girlfriend?

Preschooler:

Most preschoolers have no immediate dating plans (we'll hope!) so an answer such as "When you're 16, we'll decide" will probably suffice. You'll have time to modify that answer as you see how your child develops physically and emotionally.

Elementary-Age:

You need a family policy about early dating—when it can begin and what it looks like (in groups, only in your home, with the approval of both sets of parents, and so on). Use this question as a prompt to bring up both your dating regulations and what's behind them. Also, share that dating is a way to find the person God may have for your child to marry. Put dating in perspective for your child.

Preteen:

Your preteen may already be experimenting with "going out" at school… or online. Determine if dating has already begun—with or without your permission. Review your family's stance on dating and any rules you wish to have followed. Be aware that you'll need a reason for each; "Because I said so" won't play well with your preteen. Allow your preteen to speak into the rules (within reason), so everyone is on board. The more your preteen feels valued, the more she'll follow the rules.

Related Scriptures: With older children, read Ruth together, focusing on relationship choices. Second Corinthians 6:14 addresses dating people who don't share the Christian faith.

Q: Can girls ask out guys?

Preschooler:

Your preschooler won't ask this question, but she might ask a boy to be her boyfriend. If that happens, share that dating is for older people. Adults often think it is cute to address friends of the opposite sex as "boyfriend" and "girlfriend." Consider what message that sends to a preschooler.

Elementary-Age:

Girls often initiate asking out boys starting during early-elementary years. Encourage girls to be patient because dating is meant for later in life. Encourage boys, who seldom want much to do with girls at this age, to avoid "going out" with girls if approached. Begin thinking and praying about dating boundaries you'll give to your kids. The dating dilemma is right around the corner!

Preteen:

Be honest: There's no clear answer in the Bible—but God might well have an answer for your preteen through prayer. Encourage open dialogue about dating and begin enforcing your family's dating parameters, such as curfew, whether or not your preteen can be alone with the opposite sex, when it's okay for your preteen to have a boyfriend or girlfriend, or other rules you want to cover. Also discuss what it means to "chase boys" as well as the role your preteen's access to technology plays in her relationships. "Sexting" is a topic you must discuss if your child has a cell phone. If you haven't established parameters for dating and relationships, do so now. The earlier you start the conversation, the better.

Related Scriptures: Proverbs 4:23 speaks to guarding one's heart; Proverbs 21:23 to guarding one's tongue.

When is it okay for a girl to start wearing makeup?

Preschooler:
Your preschooler might enjoy playing with makeup, especially if she watches Mommy apply lipstick. Fine—but don't communicate she needs makeup to be beautiful to you. Your approval matters, so give it often and accompanied with hugs.

Elementary-Age:
Affirm that your daughter's natural beauty as God's wonderful creation is already remarkable, but don't expect that to satisfy her. If you've decided on an age at which makeup can be part of your daughter's life, tell her when it is. It's likely to be a few years, but you might allow your daughter to practice applying makeup on rare occasion for wear around the house. And be sure your daughter learns how to apply makeup well—in moderation. A friend who sells Mary Kay or another skin care product can teach your daughter how to use minimal makeup for maximum impact. These early foundations will help you when your daughter reaches the age to wear makeup.

Preteen:
Many of your daughter's peers are wearing makeup and it's likely your child wants to fit in, so see the advice in the paragraph above. Like it or not, your daughter seeks the approval of her friends and the attention of boys. If her mother uses makeup and she can't, expect to hear about a double standard and plan your response. Stay focused on your daughter accepting that true beauty is internal—and given by God.

Related Scriptures: First Samuel 16:7 and Proverbs 31:30 address true beauty.

Are poor people poor because they've been bad?

Preschooler:

Explain to your child that if someone doesn't have everything he needs, that doesn't make him bad. It might make him *sad*, however. Ask if your child would like to share with someone less fortunate.

Elementary-Age:

Children this age quickly notice that people have different "stuff," some more than others. Caution children about judging based on material possessions—accumulating possessions isn't how God measures goodness. It shouldn't be how we measure who's good or bad either.

Preteen:

Ask your preteen to brainstorm with you ways someone can become poor—by birth, by circumstance, through poor choices, through generously giving to others, and the like. Help your child discover that stuff doesn't equal goodness or badness. Gently probe to see if the child is concerned about possessions, or fears poverty for some reason.

Related Scriptures: Luke 6:37 addresses judging others, and James 2:2-9 the treatment of the poor. And in the "stuff" department, *Jesus* was poor (yet not bad!)—see Matthew 8:20.

If lying is wrong for me, why do you do it?

Preschooler:

Older preschoolers generally understand the difference between truth and lies…and they need you to model the importance of truth. When your preschooler sees you lie, it erodes confidence and trust. If you lie, own your mistakes, apologize, and ask forgiveness. It's a teachable moment.

Elementary-Age:

Welcome to parenting: Your behavior either supports or contradicts what you're teaching your children. If your child catches you in a lie, it's a good opportunity to help your child understand some "lies" are simple misunderstandings and others are intentional misrepresentations. If you're being challenged about the former, talk through ways to communicate better. If the latter, apologize—and let your child see you try to make amends. Humiliating? Maybe. But you're modeling integrity.

Preteen:

Preteens can sniff hypocrisy at 500 yards, and they're often quick to condemn it in others. If you expect your preteen to be open to your observations about her character, be open to her observations about yours. Respond not with defensiveness but a willingness to listen. Pray together that neither of you take shortcuts like lying—and ask for forgiveness. Your child will never forget the conversation.

Related Scriptures: Exodus 20:16 addresses lying, Proverbs 6:6-9 laziness, and 1 John 1:9 confession of sins and forgiveness.

Q: When someone says mean things about people who aren't the same color as us, is he right?

Preschooler:

No, he's wrong. God made everyone like himself and loves them just the same. We're all different—we come in different sizes and have different color skin and hair—and we're all special to God. God thinks all colors of skin are beautiful, and we should, too.

Elementary-Age:

Explain that people often judge others by the way they look, especially by skin color. Some people believe one skin color is better than others... but those people are wrong. God says he loves all his children the same. Encourage your child to look beyond skin color, height, weight, or anything that makes us different and focus on what makes us the same: We're all children of God.

Preteen:

Educate your child that in cultures throughout history, some people have judged those of a different color as being "not as good." Such thinking is wrong and has always been wrong. Judging people by skin color is called racism. Help your child learn about the Civil Rights movement, and encourage him to seek out friends who look differently than himself.

Related Scriptures: Colossians 3:10-11 states that in Jesus we're all one.

ⓠ Is trick-or-treating good or bad?

Preschooler:
If your family has a policy about Halloween, share it with your preschooler and explain why. If you don't trick-or-treat, provide a fun family alternative—and some snacks. If your little one does dress up, select a costume that honors God, rather than something that reflects evil.

Elementary-Age:
Let your elementary-age child know that people think differently about this topic, and help him seek what God would like your family to do. Help your child research the origins of Halloween online, read the Bible passages below, and pray together about whether to participate. Unless you have taken a stance against trick-or-treating, consider joining in the event with your child. You'll be on hand to keep things safe—and to avoid the dark side of the Halloween holiday.

Preteen:
It's no longer just about the candy. The costuming, the chance to be with friends...the spiritual side of Halloween may not be on your child's radar at all. With her read the passages below, and encourage her to decide for herself if she wants to participate. This is an excellent chance to let your child make a choice and prayerfully consider for herself the answer to this question.

Related Scriptures: Read together Romans 12:2; 1 Corinthians 10:23; Ephesians 5:11; 1 Thessalonians 5:21-22; and 1 John 4:3-4.

Q: Is getting a tattoo wrong?

Preschooler:

Many preschoolers have seen tattoos and worn temporary tattoos themselves. Explain that real tattoos don't wash off, are for older people, and sometimes show pictures of things God doesn't like. We should never put anything on or in our bodies that disobeys God.

Elementary-Age:

If you have an opinion concerning tattoos, tell your child. Reputable tattoo artists won't tattoo a minor, but even some elementary-age children have used ink and needles to create their own tattoos. Doing so is dangerous and foolish, with serious health risks. Tell your child anything he wears or uses as body decorating needs to obey God's Word. Ask how tattoos he's seen show love for God. If you have a tattoo you regret, share why.

Preteen:

Tattoos don't carry the social stigma they once carried, but they do send a signal—and not always one that leads to employment or acceptance. Ask your preteen to consider the counsel given by both Scripture and the experience of people who've lived with tattoos for 10 or 20 years. There's often regret for both what was tattooed and where it appears.

Related Scriptures: Leviticus 19:28 refers to marks on bodies; 1 Corinthians 6:19-20 urges us to honor God.

Is it okay to smoke since Grandma does it?

Preschooler:
Just because Grandma does it doesn't make it right. Explain to your preschooler that on every pack of cigarettes there's a warning label because smoking hurts us—and God wants us to take good care of our bodies. Explain that once you begin smoking it's very hard to stop.

Elementary-Age:
Remind your elementary-age child that older people make decisions for themselves—including the decision to smoke. However, smoking isn't good for you and doesn't take good care of the body God gave you. Most elementary-age children are already deeply opposed to smoking; encourage yours to be respectful as she expresses her opinions to her grandmother.

Preteen:
By this age your child has probably been approached about smoking—and may have tried it. Share that smoking is highly addictive and dangerous; stress that you all love Grandma, but she has put herself at great risk of disease. Assuming you want your preteen not to smoke, appeal to vanity: Smoking is both smelly and will yellow teeth. Above all, stress that God wants us to take care of our bodies, and smoking is dangerous.

Related Scriptures: First Corinthians 6:19-20 speaks to our need to honor our bodies.

Q: Why are some drugs good and some drugs bad?

Preschooler:

Talk about medicine that's helped your preschooler feel better. Describe how good drugs heal the body, yet some people take drugs that hurt their bodies. If your preschooler asks why, simply state that people don't realize how hurtful bad drugs are at the time they're taking them.

Elementary-Age:

Share that good drugs help people and bad drugs harm people. Explain good drugs are usually prescribed by doctors for a specific person and a specific reason, and they're available at stores. Bad drugs are often illegal—or are legal drugs being used illegally or that people take too much of. Explain how drugs alter one's body and mind and can become addictive. God tells us to obey the law and to take good care of our bodies! At this age, kids should only take medicine you give them.

Preteen:

Preteens understand good drugs, so spend time talking about illegal drugs and drug abuse. Explore *why* people turn to drugs, and tell your preteen God wants us to honor him with our bodies—meaning we need to take good care of them. Taking harmful drugs, or taking more medicine than the box says to take, is clearly disobeying God. Explore if your preteen is experiencing pressure to take drugs. Remind him only to take medicine when he needs it, and to follow the directions carefully.

Related Scriptures: Romans 13:1-7 urges us to obey the law; 1 Corinthians 6:19-20 and Galatians 5:19-21 stress caring for our bodies.

How come adults say bad words all the time?

Preschooler:
Remind your preschooler that adults sometimes say things that we shouldn't. Explain that adults also need help from Jesus so only good things come out their mouths.

Elementary-Age:
Communicate with your child that adults make mistakes. Some adults say bad words because they are upset or stressed. However, it's not okay for adults to say bad words any more than it's okay for children to say them. The Bible says we should only say encouraging and nice things. It's next to impossible to shield children from hearing bad words, but you *can* control what comes out of your mouth. If you need to confess and apologize, do so.

Preteen:
Some adults and even kids say bad words because they're angry or think it sounds cool. Explore together what the Bible says about cursing. Remind your preteen we need to obey God. Challenge your preteen to be an example, and encourage adults in her life to speak kind words.

Related Scriptures: Read Luke 6:45; Ephesians 4:29; and James 3:9-12 with your child. Also read 1 Timothy 4:12, a reminder that kids can be examples.

Q: If God always forgives, why do I have to do the right thing?

Preschooler:

Most preschoolers are eager to please. Tell them how happy Jesus is when we make good choices and obey him. Obeying Jesus shows that we love him. But if we do make mistakes, he'll forgive us if we ask. Together with your preschooler, ask Jesus for help in following him.

Elementary-Age:

Elementary-age children know a forced, insincere "I'm sorry" doesn't mean much. Build on that insight by asking how God must feel when someone sins and then offers up a weak "sorry" to fix the problem. Obeying God isn't a system to beat; it's a choice to live our best and to show God love. Help your child see forgiveness as a way of setting things right with God when we make mistakes—but it's not a license to sin. The passages below will help.

Preteen:

Your preteen already knows right from wrong—but still requires help making healthy decisions. Practice thinking ahead, weighing the benefits of making a good choice against the consequences of making a bad one. Talk about why making a good choice shows love for God. Actively praise your child when he makes good choices. Model forgiveness when the choices aren't good.

Related Scriptures: Hebrews 10:19-22 and 1 John 1:9 assure us of forgiveness, but Romans 6:1-2 warns us to not continue to intentionally sin.

If you have an eating disorder, does that mean you're bad?

Preschooler:
It's unlikely your preschooler will ask but, if she does, share that eating disorders are illnesses—and doctors can help. If your preschooler seems overly concerned about her weight, consider how much emphasis you put on appearances in your home. For the most part, preschoolers reflect what they observe around them.

Elementary-Age:
Assure your child that people with eating disorders aren't bad. They have pain in their lives...pain they're dealing with in ways that may be harmful to their bodies. Talk with your child about how only God can truly heal pain in our lives, but doctors can help. Find out why your child is asking, and get help if needed.

Preteen:
People who have eating disorders aren't bad—they're just human. And their problem is life-threatening. If this question arises, use it to prompt a discussion with your preteen. Does she have friends who struggle with eating disorders? Has she binged or purged to control weight gain herself? Don't interrogate, but do assure your preteen that if the issue arises for her, she'll find you both supportive and caring—and you'll assist her in getting help.

Related Scriptures: The Bible doesn't specifically address eating disorders, but it does address self-worth (Matthew 10:29-31), depression (John 16:33), and perfectionism (1 John 1:8-10)—often root causes of eating disorders.

Q: Is an abortion killing a baby?

Preschooler:

This may be a scary concept for preschoolers, so tread lightly. Carefully help your preschooler understand that some babies die before they are born for various reasons. Some preschoolers may express sadness—pray with your preschooler and assure him that God takes care of these babies.

Elementary-Age:

Be sensitive and cautious. This conversation could be traumatic. Discuss why women have abortions. Don't accuse or judge…but help your child understand that people try to make the best decision possible, even if those decisions are wrong. Say that God makes a baby inside a woman's belly, and abortion means the baby won't be born. Allow your child to express his feelings. Pray together.

Preteen:

Preteens are old enough to understand why abortion is a hot topic. Explain both pro-life and pro-choice arguments. Discover together what the Bible says about unborn babies (see references below). It's clear that God values life while babies are in the womb, and abortion takes that life. Be careful not to condemn people for having different beliefs about abortion than yours. This is a chance to encourage your child to have compassion and love for people. Remind him that God forgives and loves people, and we should, too.

Related Scriptures: See Psalm 139 and Jeremiah 1:5.

Is lying okay if it helps someone feel good?

Preschooler:
Explain God wants us to tell the truth—and your child can do so in a kind way. If he doesn't want to play with someone, he can simply say, "I don't want to play now" without making up an excuse, which is really a lie.

Elementary-Age:
Explain that character is important. We're all good at justifying lying, and that's the dark side of this issue. Explain that the truth can be told in a harsh or loving way—but sharing the truth is always the right thing to do. If there's a specific situation prompting this question, brainstorm with your child how he can tell the truth in a loving way.

Preteen:
Seeing Dad lie to Mom about looking good in a new dress doesn't help with this one, does it? If lying is a routine part of how you communicate in your home, address that. For example, Dad could say, "I like your green dress better; it brings out your eyes." Modeling loving truth-telling will have the biggest impact on your preteen. And if your preteen asks, tell her God wants us to be kind in the way we tell the truth rather than lying to protect someone. Talk about specific ideas for doing that if your child is dealing with a specific situation.

Related Scriptures: Read Proverbs 12:22 and Proverbs 19:9 to see God's view of lying; refer to Proverbs 30:8 to discover what ours should be.

Q: Why don't we have as much money as my friend's family?

Preschooler:
Preschoolers may notice that others have more toys or bigger houses. Help children see the many blessings God has given *them*. Point out their food, toys, clothes, and family. With your child, thank God throughout the day. Help your child know there are others who have more need than you. Donate some of your things.

Elementary-Age:
Children need to understand that more money isn't always better, and real wealth isn't just money. God blesses us with family, health, time, and love. Help your child not be jealous of what others have, but to appreciate what God has given her. Make a "blessing list" with your child. Remind her God wants us to seek joy from our friendship with him above all material things, and that comparing ourselves with others doesn't help us be joyful.

Preteen:
There's nothing wrong with having money and using it wisely, but God warns us not to seek after anything more than we seek after him. God provides us with what we need, not necessarily what we want. Remind preteens that God wants us to seek joy from our relationship with him— not from material things. Your child may be making other comparisons to friends, such as physical appearance or number of friends. Talk about that and remind your child that finding joy is hard when we compare ourselves to others.

Related Scriptures: Philippians 4:19 promises God will meet our needs. Deuteronomy 8:18 shows that wealth comes from God.

Why does my friend have two mommies?

Preschooler:
Understanding family roles is especially important to preschoolers. Explain that God is happy when children have people who love and care for them, but God's first choice is that all children have one mommy and one daddy.

Elementary-Age:
Acknowledge that children live in a variety of family settings, but God designed families to have a mother and father. Explain that although God loves the two mommies, God says it's wrong for two girls or two boys to act like a married couple. Remind children we should love others like God loves us, and it's important to treat everyone with kindness.

Preteen:
Preteens become familiar with homosexuality through the media, your community, and other students. Homosexuality is sometimes condoned socially, and some popular TV shows and school clubs promote it. On the other hand, some kids tease people who are gay or who have homosexual parents. Help your child clearly understand God's preference for families consisting of a father and mother and sexual activity only being appropriate within marriage. Also, remind your child that God does not want us to ever hate others, and that we shouldn't tease or bully anyone.

Related Scriptures: Hebrews 13:4 speaks to the honor of marriage. Leviticus 18:22, 24 tells of God's desire for man and woman to be together.

Q: Why do people fake being your friend?

Preschooler:

Help your preschooler make friends and be a good friend herself. Emphasize sharing, caring, and being sensitive to others' feelings. Share that we can be a friend to others like Jesus is a friend to us. And assure your child that even when other friends are selfish and not good friends, Jesus will always be our best friend.

Elementary-Age:

During the elementary years your child will discover not everyone will want to be her friend. Worse: Some people will pretend to be friendly because they want something. Explain that friends are made—and proven true—over time. If your child's feelings are hurt by a false friendship, comfort her and assure her she's got a life-long friend in you—and in God.

Preteen:

Let your preteen know that some people will pretend they like you if they want something from you. Your preteen can watch for friends like that and try to only choose true friends. If your child is struggling to make and keep friends, be aware that the common denominator in each friendship is your child. Consider books, counselors, or other resources to help your child sort out how to maintain friendships. Also take care to put her in situations where she can meet friends who will build her up, not tear her down. Check out youth groups and service clubs.

Related Scriptures: Jeremiah 17:9 speaks to our deceitful hearts. Proverbs 17:17; Ecclesiastes 4:9-12; and John 15:13 describe true friendships.

If you love mommy/daddy, why do you always fight?

Preschooler:
Preschoolers crave security and safety—beginning at home. If your child asks this question, tell him that even grown-ups disagree sometimes. God wants us to be nice when we disagree, but sometimes even mommies and daddies mess up. Offer a sincere apology. Also consider why the question was asked. How are you communicating around your child? What are you saying to your child about how love looks?

Elementary-Age:
Your child learns to communicate at home; what she sees will be reflected and amplified in her life…and, eventually, in her marriage. If your child sees ongoing conflict and tension in your marriage, address that reality. Share that you and your spouse are working on resolving your disagreements—and do it. And seek to *never* put your child in the middle of your disputes.

Preteen:
How you treat the other parent of your child when you're angry is a model of conflict resolution for your child. Choose to be as loving and Christlike as possible. Does that mean faking your feelings? No…but it does mean demonstrating the restraint you expect in your preteen. And let your child *see* you taking steps to resolve your differences with the other parent.

Related Scriptures: Matthew 5:22-24 speaks to God's intent that we resolve conflicts, and Romans 12:18 how we should live.

Q: When you were little, what did you do that got you in trouble?

Preschooler:

Here's a chance to connect with your little one—and show that everyone makes mistakes. Even if it's embarrassing, share that you, too, got in trouble—and what you learned from your mistakes. Your child is still young, so give examples that won't introduce new ways to misbehave.

Elementary-Age:

If you've stayed silent about what mistakes you made at your child's age, consider sharing some of that information. It's a teaching opportunity—and the chance to bond with your child. It's okay to appear human to your child; handled properly it won't provide permission to make the same mistakes you made! Here's an example to get your juices flowing: "When I was 8, I broke something by accident. But I was embarrassed, so I lied to my parents. My mom eventually caught me and I learned that telling the truth would have been better for me and my parents."

Preteen:

Every generation of preteens believes they're the first to experience the uncertainty of transition into adulthood. Not so—and by opening up about your life, you can provide valuable coaching and insight. Be careful not to slip into a "friend" role; your child needs the security of your staying in your parental role. It's possible to share from your own life and still be respected as a parent. Share your experience and talk about the consequences. Use the example above to get you started.

Related Scriptures: Share these passages with your child: Proverbs 22:6; Ecclesiastes 1:9; and 1 Corinthians 13:11. Then share a few stories.

Why do my church friends act just like my friends who don't go to church?

Preschooler:

Preschoolers are unlikely to make this distinction, but note: Preschoolers have a way of being themselves no matter where they are. Avoid forcing your preschooler to be one way at church and allowing her to be another way elsewhere. "Being good only while at church" sets up double standards.

Elementary-Age:

Acknowledge that going to church doesn't make someone a Christian. It doesn't even necessarily change a person's behavior. Your child is old enough to understand there's a difference between following Jesus and going to church, obeying rules, and saying the right words. Encourage your child to follow Jesus, letting him guide her behavior. She doesn't have to be like her church friends whose lives don't reflect God's values.

Preteen:

Ask your preteen how she thinks Christians should act…and what influences them to act otherwise. What does your preteen think fuels authentic life change that's visible? Rather than deliver judgment, suggest your preteen be an example—to both churched and unchurched friends.

Related Scriptures: Read and discuss Romans 2:13; 3:22-24; and James 1:22-24.

If people don't know about Jesus, how do I tell them?

Preschooler:
Preschoolers talk about what they know and learn. So if you're talking about Jesus, they're talking about Jesus. Little ones can tell others by saying, "Jesus loves you," sharing a book about Jesus with a friend, or inviting a friend to church.

Elementary-Age:
Many elementary children will openly tell others about Jesus. At this age, they firmly believe what their parents believe. They may openly ask others if they know Jesus and be worried for those who don't. Help your child practice telling her faith story, including when, how, and why she decided to follow Jesus. Also encourage your child to share Jesus through her actions, by being a good friend, and by helping others.

Preteen:
It's often scary for preteens to talk to people about Jesus, especially friends. Preteens are still developing their own relationship with Jesus. They also worry about what others will think of them. Fitting in is huge to preteens. If your child is worried about being teased for being a Christian, encourage her that teasing means people are seeing Jesus in her—and that's a good thing! She may express concern for a non-Christian. Let your child know that our actions tell about Jesus as well as our verbal sharing.

Related Scriptures: Matthew 28:19 is a good verse about discipleship for older kids. John 13:34-35 tells us to love others.

Q: How come my friends are mean to me?

Preschooler:

The preschool years are all about learning social skills. Ask what your child means by "being mean" and listen carefully. Your child may have been teased, had a friend who didn't share, or had a friend who hurt him. Determine if this is a report of growing pains or bullying. Use the situation as an opportunity to explore what it means to be a good friend as you read Proverbs 17:17 together.

Elementary-Age:

Because healthy relationships are a critical component in your child's development, it's important to help your child discern who's a good friend and who's not. Ask questions about what happened and help your child determine if he's been a good friend in this situation. Then discuss how he can go about resolving the dispute. If bullying is occurring, get involved. Talk to your school or church leaders about the bullying. Teach your child how to avoid physical conflict but still stand up for himself.

Preteen:

You can't manage your preteen's relationships—and probably shouldn't, if they're normal and healthy—but you *can* help your preteen discover how his communication style and expectations might be contributing to the issue. If your preteen reports all his friends are mean, there's likely one of two things going on: bullying on the friends' part or unrealistic expectations on your preteen's part. Help your preteen work on making and maintaining relationships. And if bullying is present, get involved.

Related Scriptures: Explore God's take on friendship with these passages: Proverbs 17:17; Matthew 7:12; and 1 Peter 4:8.

Q: Why don't you like my friends?

Preschooler:

It's hard not to like preschoolers—they're so cute! If you don't like one of your child's friends, the issue is probably the other child's actions. Explain to your child you do like his friend, but not everything that child does. Identify those actions; this is a great training opportunity for your child, too.

Elementary-Age:

Don't deny your feelings; they're evident or your child wouldn't be asking you this question. Be descriptive and specific rather than judgmental regarding what behaviors and attitudes you don't appreciate in your child's friend, such as rudeness or selfishness. Give examples of when the friend has exhibited those characteristics. If you've seen those behaviors reflected in your child, gently indicate that as well.

Preteen:

This question may be more of an accusation than an actual question. Don't take the bait; if you forbid contact then your child's friend becomes even more desirable. Be nonjudgmental as you describe the behaviors or attitudes you don't find attractive in your child's friend. Ask how your child deals with those attributes, too, but don't force your child to choose between you and his friend.

Related Scriptures: We become like our friends—see Proverbs 13:20. Proverbs 22:24 also offers insight about picking friends.

Q: Why don't I have more friends?

Preschooler:

Your child *can* have more friends—if she does what it takes to have them. Help your child practice being kind and inclusive. And calm her by naming family and friends she already has—people who love her now. Consider setting up play dates to help your child practice playing with friends.

Elementary-Age:

In one moment elementary-age kids show self-awareness, kindness, and empathy. The next moment they ignore everyone in the room. Practice skills with your child that initiate and build friendships: listening, sharing, and being attentive to what others need. To have friends, your child needs to be a good friend. And remind your child that friends aren't guaranteed to last; it takes effort to keep friends once friendships are struck.

Preteen:

Your preteen may measure friends by how many are connected through social media. Help your preteen discover that a few close, real friends are far more important than hundreds of barely-connected contacts online. Making and keeping friends requires commitment and effort. How much is your preteen giving to cultivating and keeping friends? Consider helping your child join a service organization, youth group, or a team sport, or find school-based drama or band opportunities.

Related Scriptures: Having more friends isn't as important as having the right friends. Read Proverbs 12:26; 18:24; and Ecclesiastes 4:10.

Fears

Q: Why am I afraid of the dark?

Preschooler:

This one's simple: We often fear the dark because we can't see very well in it. So illuminate your child's feelings with a safe and loving environment and a little extra lighting. Nightlights help, as do bedtime rituals that assure and comfort your preschooler. Read a story, cuddle, and pray together. Let your preschooler know that fears are normal, but God can help us when we're afraid.

Elementary-Age:

Explain fear is an emotion—and she needn't be ashamed she's afraid of the dark. But we *can* control fear, and she can conquer this one. Install a dimmer switch on a lamp and slowly reduce light in the room; allow your child to set the pace with a mutual goal in mind. Ask what your child fears (fire? burglars? monsters?) and address those during daylight by making plans to help with those fears, such as making a fire escape plan, checking locks and alarm system, or discussing how we know monsters aren't real. And pray together at bedtime—invite God into this process.

Preteen:

Being afraid of the dark is one thing. Being afraid after a marathon of slasher movies is another. Encourage your preteen to make wise decisions about fueling her imagination. If your preteen is experiencing night frights, it may be an indication of something else happening in her life. During the day, ask about what might be concerning her at school, with friends, and at home.

Related Scriptures: Read Psalm 56:3-4; Philippians 4:13; 2 Timothy 1:7; and 1 John 4:18 with your child.

Q: If we move, will I have friends there?

Preschooler:
Moving is exciting for some preschoolers and scary for others—not so different from adults. Affirm your preschooler's feelings, and admit you'll both miss friends if you move. Assure your child you'll both make more friends in your new location, and best of all: God is with you wherever you go.

Elementary-Age:
Explaining *why* you're moving may ease some of your child's anxiety. Assure your child that, in time, she'll make new friends at school, in the neighborhood, or through extra-curricular activities. Help your child take her worries and feelings to God in prayer. Remind your child God is with you wherever you go.

Preteen:
The older the child, the harder the idea of moving. If you moved as a child, share your experiences. Your goal: to help your preteen open up about worries and to provide reassurance at the same time. Assure your preteen that she'll make new friends—just as she has through other transitions. Pray together. Remind your preteen God already knows who her new friends will be…and that she can maintain current friendships through letters, calls, and texts.

Related Scriptures: Read Joshua 1:9 for courage. Psalm 139:1-3 reassures us that God knows us and our situation.

When are you getting a divorce?

These answers assume you're not in the process of divorcing. If you are divorcing, provide reassurance of your love.

Preschooler:

Tell your preschooler you're not getting a divorce. Preschoolers may ask this because they fear losing one or more parents—or because they're hoping for double the amount of Christmas presents (it's happened!). Reassure your child of your love and the stability of your home life.

Elementary-Age:

An elementary-age child may be responding to conflict in your home— especially between parents. He may interpret arguments between parents as a signal of a coming divorce. Take this as an opportunity to reassure your child of your love for each other (and him). Apologize to your child for any arguments you've had with your spouse in front of him. Let him know you and your spouse need to resolve conflicts calmly, but sometimes you mess up and get angry. Try to keep your arguments behind closed doors in the future.

Preteen:

Preteens may not understand marriage is a commitment—one that needs to weather both good times and bad. Explain how you're working through a difficult circumstance. Acknowledge that your marriage isn't perfect, but you're making it better because you love each other and your family. Model the marriage you hope your children will one day enjoy.

Related Scriptures: See 1 Corinthians 7:10 regarding commitment in marriage and 1 Peter 4:8 regarding the importance of love.

Q: Should I run from a bully?

Preschooler:

Bullying starts early—and so should learning appropriate responses. Practice with your preschooler two responses: First, report bullying to adults (including you) immediately. It's not "tattling." And second, confront bullies verbally; it usually prompts them to stop. Suggest your child say, "I'm sorry I made you angry, but I don't want to fight."

Elementary-Age:

Your elementary-age child may well face a social stigma if she "tells" on a bully. However, it's okay to get teachers and other adults involved if the bullying continues or becomes physical in any way. Teach your child to *never* bully others; encourage her to *always* stand up for herself if she's bullied in person or through social media. Urge her to also stand up for others being bullied—it will continue if bystanders don't get involved. Encourage your child to gather friends and act brave and confident with bullies, and to say in a loud voice, "No! Stop it!" if a bully is bothering her.

Preteen:

Bullying comes in many forms: physical, verbal, social, and cyber. Tell your preteen it takes courage to confront bullies—and sometimes that courage is in turning bullies in to authorities. Your preteen may also thwart bullying by showing kindness. Bullies are usually mean because they're troubled, and by showing kindness rather than acting like a victim, your preteen could stay away from harm and help someone at the same time. Thank your preteen for telling you what's going on—and check in often.

Related Scriptures: See Leviticus 19:18 about revenge and 2 Timothy 1:7 regarding living a fearful life.

Q: How come terrorists want to kill us?

Preschooler:

Your preschooler doesn't understand political or religious ideology—but he does understand that people are different. Explain some people want to hurt those who are different from them and you're doing everything you can to keep your preschooler safe. Rather than worry about terrorists, suggest you and your preschooler pray that God helps them see hurting people is wrong.

Elementary-Age:

Your elementary child may fear for her safety—or simply be overwhelmed that an unknown enemy wants to hurt her. Tell your child that some people are terrorists because they don't like people who are different from them. Do some research together to help her see that there are not, in fact, many terrorists. Remind her not to return hate for hate. This is an opportunity to do as Jesus taught: Love those who hate you.

Preteen:

Help your preteen grasp some details regarding the political, social, and economic reasons that terrorism exists. But even with additional details, you'll still need to assure your preteen that she doesn't need to fear terrorism. Rather, she needs to pray for those who participate in terrorist activities.

Related Scriptures: Jesus encourages us to pray for our enemies in Matthew 5:44, and Psalm 27:1 reminds us of God's protection.

Q: Will I get saggy like you when I get old?

Preschooler:
Ah, parenthood—the very individual who's contributed most to your "sag" now questions you about it! The answer is probably "yes," but assure your child that by eating well and playing active games she can avoid excessive sagging. Suggest you skip TV for a day and play fun, active games together instead.

Elementary-Age:
Share that some "sagging" is inevitable, but if your child makes healthy choices about food and activity, she can avoid obesity—which is epidemic. Ask if she's willing to take on more responsibility concerning her choices and, if so, what choices she'd like to make. And, of course, do your best to not be discouraged about what might have prompted the question.

Preteen:
Your preteen might be asking this question out of her concern about body image, beauty, and appearance. This is a wonderful opportunity to discuss both having a positive body image in spite of perceived flaws, and also taking responsibility for healthy choices that help avoid sagging. Explore also if your preteen has concerns about your health and the choices you're making.

Related Scriptures: Exodus 20:12 suggests one way to live long. And age has benefits: See Job 12:12.

Q: If I have ADD, am I broken?

Preschooler:
Being labeled can be a heartbreaking thing. Your child is looking to you to give meaning to any label stuck on him by friends, the school system, even the church. Help your child see that attention-deficit disorder isn't a problem; it's one difference among many. Encourage and accept and be clear: You're not broken.

Elementary-Age:
Hold your child close as you explain: "God doesn't make broken people; God makes people who have a huge variety of differences. ADD is one of those." Promise to be there for your child, through ADD, through learning to drive, through all of life's challenges. And as he discovers his unique God-given gifts.

Preteen:
ADD can create significant challenges in academic settings. Be certain if your child has ADD by getting a reliable diagnosis. Consider medication, but with or without medication draw your child close and together brainstorm how to overcome the challenges ADD presents at school, at home, at church, and elsewhere. Share with your child you love him just as he is—and so does the God who made him just as he is.

Related Scriptures: See Jeremiah 1:5 and Revelation 4:11—reassuring words that no child is an afterthought.

Q: Mommy, Daddy—when will you die?

Preschooler:
Since you don't know when you'll die, don't make promises...though you can assure your child that you want to be with him when he goes to school, gets married, and has children of his own. Focus on your hope of a shared future together. Make a will and appoint a guardian for your child.

Elementary-Age:
By now your child knows about death and the separation it brings. If your child's question is prompted by your health, be honest—and focus on your shared eternity together in heaven. If he is fearful about what would happen to him in the event of your death, share the guardianship plans you've made. Assure your child you'll be waiting for him in heaven should you die.

Preteen:
Help your child feel safe. Share stories of loved ones your family has lost and your certainty of a future together in heaven. Tell your child about guardianship plans in place. Yes, we'll all die...but death isn't the end for people who love Jesus.

Related Scriptures: God wants the best for your child—see Jeremiah 29:11. And worrying about death doesn't change it—see Matthew 6:27.

Q: Will the world blow up soon?

Preschooler:

You preschooler is less afraid about the world ending than *her* world ending. Remind her that God cares for her and your family. We don't know what will happen, but we know God is in control. Share stories from the Bible about how God can protect people he loves. The life of David is a great place to begin. (See 1 Samuel 17:8-58.)

Elementary-Age:

Will this world end? Yes—but Jesus predicted as much and it's part of his healing of creation. Encourage your child to daily seek to know God, be following God, and value what God values. God is in control, not nations.

Preteen:

Why go to school if you expect the world to detonate tomorrow? Because we don't know how or when this world will end. Only God knows that. Remind your child that God wants for all people to be able to hear about Jesus and is sustaining the world so that can happen. God's plan is to save all those who choose to be saved—and the end of this world is nothing to fear for those who know God.

Related Scriptures: We can trust in God's protection—see Psalm 91:2. And see 2 Peter 3:9 to learn God's intent for all to know him.

Q: Do you ever get scared, too?

Preschooler:
It's not appropriate for you to confess all your fears to your preschooler; she finds comfort in your strength. But you can say that everyone is afraid sometimes—even you. Assure your child it's okay to be afraid, but God can take those fears away because he's strong and he loves your child. Consider sharing a story of fear from your childhood and how God helped you. Pray with your child.

Elementary-Age:
Never brush off your child's fears. Rather, affirm it's *not* bad we get scared—even you get scared sometimes. It *is* a problem when we run away from our fears rather than letting God help us conquer them. Pray with your child, asking God to walk through her fears with her. Also, be sure the media your child consumes isn't fueling those fears.

Preteen:
Preteens crave affirmation that they're normal—including knowing others get scared, too. Share how God has helped you with fears, and point your preteen to Jesus, who may have been scared as he waited in the garden to be taken away and killed. Jesus chose to trust God rather than fear—a decision your child can make, too.

Related Scriptures: God doesn't intend for us to live in fear—see 2 Timothy 1:7; Hebrews 13:6; and 1 Peter 5:7.

Q: Are we ever going to be homeless?

Preschooler:

Share that God is mindful of—and provides for—our needs. And encourage your preschooler to think of "home" as more than a physical location; it's also the people God has put in our lives.

Elementary-Age:

Whatever prompted this question should be the focus of your answer. Ask your child why he is asking the question. Are you suffering from a job loss or recent divorce that hurt your finances? Without giving details, let your child know you'll be making fewer purchases. Enlist your child in helping control expenses and cutting coupons.

Preteen:

Be as open as you can about your financial situation without going into detail. If there's a change, make your preteen aware of it. Otherwise, your child will pick up on the fear and not know the plan. Model a primary dependence on God; as a person and as a parent, turn first to God and rely on him. What you say will matter, and what you model will transform your child's life.

Related Scriptures: Jesus puts our possessions in perspective in Luke 9:57-59; 12:22-24. And Psalm 56:3-4 and Proverbs 3:5-7 encourage us to trust God.

Q: How come I keep having nightmares?

Preschooler:
Nightmares often spring from fear and, occasionally, from spiritual attack. Well before bedtime, talk with your child about what fears may be bothering her. Avoid things that contribute to those fears. Then pray with your preschooler before she sleeps. Read Bible verses with your child (see below) and assure her God is with her even while she sleeps.

Elementary-Age:
Ask your child to share what happens in her dream and, together, explore what fears might be prompting the dream. At this age your child may be able to articulate her fears and concerns. Pray with and for your child, especially before she goes to bed. Let your child know that dreams are often based on something that happened during the day. Help your child process negative things that happen each day so they won't plague her dreams.

Preteen:
Pray with your preteen, too, but also talk with your child about the "input" into her imagination. What sort of television programs, movies, and Internet sites are feeding her mental images? How might limiting (or eliminating) those influences improve her ability to sleep peacefully? If cutting negative input doesn't help, have your preteen write out what happens in her nightmares—then rewrite it so it's not scary. Before going to bed, your preteen can visualize the rewritten version of the dream to help aid her sleep.

Related Scriptures: See these passages: Psalm 4:8; 34:4; and Proverbs 3:24. Second Timothy 1:7 speaks to our spirit of fear.

Q: How do I know for sure I'm a Christian?

Preschooler:
Share that a Christian is someone who loves and follows Jesus. Help your preschooler express her love for Jesus, and pray with her.

Elementary-Age:
Kids sometimes think they're Christians because they go to church or because their parents are Christians. Clarify you're a Christian if you've given your life to Jesus by telling him you want to live for him. You're still someone who makes mistakes, but you're a Christian and your doubts don't erase that relationship with God through Jesus.

Preteen:
Preteens are in the process of owning their faith, which involves questioning concepts they once accepted as truth. It's normal to doubt, question, and explore, so *don't panic*. Affirm that seeking truth is a healthy process, and trust that honest exploration will lead your preteen to God through Jesus. Offer encouragement and support…and pray without ceasing. Closing down exploration doesn't remove doubts—it just removes you from a position in which you can speak into your preteen's searching for God.

Related Scriptures: Even John the Baptist and Thomas wrestled with doubt—see Matthew 11:1-6 and John 20:24-29. And see 1 John 5:13 and 2 Timothy 1:12.

Q: If I'm good, will God love me more?

Preschooler:

Tempting to say "yes," isn't it, to prompt obedience? But don't. You're a model of God's love for your child, and God's love isn't performance-based. Does he love us when we're good? Yes. When we're bad? Yes. Did he love us enough to send Jesus *before* we were good? Yes.

Elementary-Age:

Use this as a chance to discuss and explore the characteristics of God—and your child's response to God. Psalm 136 will help your child know God loves him no matter what. Being good or bad doesn't change how God loves us, but being good shows God we love him.

Preteen:

If you've believed—or *still* believe—that God loves you more when you're good, share your story with your child. Assure your child no matter how tempting it is to believe good behavior wins God's affection, it's not true. We don't obey God because it makes him love us more; we obey as a loving response because he *already* loves us—and we wish to please him. God's nature is unchanging. When we grow closer to God, it's we who change, not God.

Related Scriptures: Read Romans 5:8 and John 3:16 to confirm that God loves us—period! How can God show his love more than by sending Jesus?

Q: Why does God let people die?

Preschooler:

Preschoolers are learning to deal with separation—*Mommy comes back when she leaves me*—and may not understand the permanency of physical death. They *do* understand sadness and someone going away. Explain God is sad when we're sad, and people who know Jesus go to heaven to be with God.

Elementary-Age:

Following a death, elementary-age children may be scared they will die, too. Reassure your child that although death on earth means the person is absent from us, he's present with God. It's hard when we can't be with someone we love, but one day we'll be together in heaven. It's okay to be sad or even angry at God.

Preteen:

Preteens can understand that God never wanted death. Death is a result of sin and, since we're all sinners, God sent Jesus so we can have eternal life. People who know Christ go to heaven. Although we're sad someone we love dies, we have to trust God. It's hard to understand that our time on earth is insignificant compared to our eternal life in a perfect place forever.

Related Scriptures: Ephesians 2:8-9 says God saved us through grace and we accept it through faith.

Q: Who made God?

Preschooler:
Most preschoolers will be satisfied if you simply say no one made God. Only things that have a beginning, like toys, have to be made. Since God didn't have a beginning, he didn't need anyone to make him.

Elementary-Age:
Strap yourself in for a romp through science, theology, and philosophy. There's *plenty* you could study and discuss, but the answer really comes down to faith and believing God has always been around. Honor the question, but bring your child back around to Jesus, who considered God eternal. If Jesus is real—and right—his teaching about God is the same.

Preteen:
This question is sometimes tossed at Christian preteens to attack their faith. If your preteen is asking this question, he might feel he needs a rational answer or his faith is a sham. Reassure your child there are some things about God we simply can't understand. We know God has always been around and there was no beginning to God's life, even if that's hard to understand. Some things we take on faith—trusting that the God we know can be bigger than the answers we find so comforting.

Related Scriptures: Read Isaiah 40:28; 55:8-11; Psalm 90:2; Romans 16:26; and 1 Timothy 1:17.

Q: Is God the boss of Jesus?

Preschooler:
The Trinity is a tough concept for preschoolers, so simply say that God is in charge of everything—and Jesus did as God told him. We should do the same.

Elementary-Age:
Explain that God the Father is above all, and Jesus followed the Father's will. That doesn't mean Jesus is inferior; they're co-equal. An example: A Christian wife may submit to her husband, but she's not inferior. She simply has one role and he has another.

Preteen:
Explain that God, Jesus, and the Holy Spirit share some important attributes: None of them were created. All are creators. All are eternal. They're equal but express themselves through different roles: Father, Son, and Guide. In short, God isn't Jesus' boss...but Jesus has submitted to God's guidance. They are one voice and one spirit.

Related Scriptures: Read John 10:30; 14:10; and Revelation 22:13.

Does God get mad if we eat without praying first?

Preschooler:

No, God doesn't get angry—but he *does* want us to be thankful for what we receive from him. Just before we eat is a great time to be thankful!

Elementary-Age:

Nowhere in the Bible are Christ-followers told to pause before eating to pray. There are examples of Jesus doing so (see the passages below) but no requirement we do the same. The larger point: We need to remain thankful for blessings God gives us—and meals are an easy time to express that thankfulness. Ask your child how to make prayer before meals meaningful rather than rote. If prayers have become just habit, they're not honoring God.

Preteen:

Your preteen might be embarrassed to bow his head and pray before eating—at least in the school cafeteria. Stress that while prayer isn't required at those moments, our heartfelt thankfulness is...even for cafeteria food. Ask what your child might want to do rather than pray to express his gratitude to God. Or perhaps your child will consider a brief prayer a witness to those around him.

Related Scriptures: See Matthew 14:19; 15:36; and 26:27 for examples of Jesus praying. Read James 1:17 for a reminder of where blessings originate.

If God listens when I pray, why doesn't he answer?

Preschooler:
Assure your preschooler God always listens to our prayers but, just like a parent, he doesn't always say "yes" and give us what we request.

Elementary-Age:
Share that the Bible teaches God always answers prayers—but not always the way we want. Also, God wants us to pray with confidence that he's there...and that he cares. Prayer isn't like a request process; it's a relationship. Explore what prayers your child feels aren't being answered. Perhaps the answers have been given—but not noticed or received by your child. Pray with your child, and pray specifically so you can see God answer.

Preteen:
Using the passages below, help your preteen discover that effective prayer requires something on her part, too. She must pray in faith, with the right motives, and without unconfessed sin. Also, be sure your preteen understands that God knows so much more than we do, and he answers prayers in the way that's ultimately best—even if it's not what we want.

Related Scriptures: Read about prayer in Isaiah 59:1-2; Matthew 21:22; John 15:7; and James 1:6-8; 4:3.

How come God gets to do whatever he wants to do?

Preschooler:
Because your preschooler lives in a world where she gets to make very few choices, that God gets to tell even *parents* what to do must be amazing! Explain that God's rules are all for our good, and help us live better lives. God's rules help us love him and other people better.

Elementary-Age:
Assure your child that while God gets to make the rules, he does so carefully—and does nothing that's not motivated by love. And unlike rules delivered by parents and other authority figures, God's rules are unchanging. Together discuss this: Why has God done what he's done? What's he trying to accomplish? Help your child discover for himself that God is all about having a good relationship with his creation.

Preteen:
Preteens are old enough to know that with great authority comes great responsibility. God does what he chooses, but he gives great thought to how his actions affect his creation. His main purpose is to lovingly restore us to a perfect relationship with him.

Related Scriptures: God's in charge, but it requires something from him—see Luke 12:48.

Sometimes in the Bible God seems mean. Why?

Preschooler:
Help your preschooler know the difference between being mean and providing discipline so we don't get hurt. God is love—and is never mean. Never. But like a parent, God disciplines us when we need it. His goal: to bring us closer to him.

Elementary-Age:
Your elementary-age child is old enough to connect consequences with her actions. Ask your child what she'd expect you, as a parent, to do if she were to break your family's rules. What does she think your motive would be for providing discipline? God corrects his children not because he's mean, but because he loves them and knows what's best to keep people from getting hurt.

Preteen:
Your preteen is sorting out what he thinks of God. If he's reading portions of the Bible that deal with punishment, he may be seeing them for the first time; Sunday school lessons seldom cover those passages. Help your preteen see God not as mean but as just—and as a parent who values his children enough to risk their displeasure by providing punishment. Even when we don't understand God's actions, we can trust he's doing the right thing because God is always good. God might seem mean simply because we don't understand what he's doing, but we can trust that he's always motivated by love.

Related Scriptures: God's discipline is loving—see Psalm 94:12; Proverbs 13:24; and Hebrews 12:6.

Q: Does God ever talk to people out loud so they can hear him?

Preschooler:

Write a note to your preschooler and offer to read it to her. Tell her that often God speaks to his people through the Bible—his giant note to the world. Yes, God can speak out loud...but he usually uses the Bible.

Elementary-Age:

The short answer: Yes...though God usually "speaks" through the Bible. Your child may be wondering why, if God wants us to do what he wants, he doesn't just *tell* us what he wants...audibly. After all, that's what parents do! But God also speaks to us through our hearts sometimes. Ask your child if she wants to hear God's voice speaking to her and, if she does, pray together that she'll always have a heart that is listening for God's voice.

Preteen:

Yes, God can speak audibly—the Bible documents examples of that happening and some Christians report hearing God speak. But having that experience doesn't mean someone is more spiritual than others. Through the Holy Spirit, God speaks into the lives of all Christians. What sets some Christians apart is that they actually *listen*—and *obey*. Ask your child if she's willing to obey when God speaks to her through the Bible or within her heart.

Related Scriptures: God speaks through the Bible (2 Timothy 3:16-17) and the Holy Spirit (John 16:13).

Why doesn't God stop bad stuff from happening to us?

Preschooler:
When hard things happen in your preschooler's life, hold her close. Remind her God loves her and is with her—just as you're with her. Let your child know that even though God can do anything, sometimes he lets people make choices, and those can hurt other people.

Elementary-Age:
Could God stop bad things from happening? Yes. Does he? Not always. Explain to your child that bad things happen because people do bad things—sin has entered the picture. If God removed our freedom to do things that lead to painful consequences, we'd be no more than robots, programmed to obey God. God wants a loving relationship with us—and that requires he give us choices. It also means that other people have choices, so they have the opportunity to choose to sin, which often hurts us.

Preteen:
Share that we all have choices, and we don't always make the right ones. Your preteen can share some examples she's seen of just that. Point out that God doesn't dictate our choices because he wants us to choose to love and obey him. The downside: The consequences of our choices—and choices made by others—often lead to pain.

Related Scriptures: Joshua 24:15 and Matthew 11:28 speak to our making good choices, and John 16:33 is a reminder that Jesus is ultimately in control.

Does God watch me even when I'm in the bathroom?

Preschooler:

If you've not already established rules regarding modesty and privacy, this is a *great* time. Share with your child that while God can always see us, he already knows everything about us, so we don't need to be embarrassed.

Elementary-Age:

The word is *omnipresence:* God's ability to be everywhere at once. That God's always with us is a *good* thing—not one that should prompt shame or embarrassment. Consider, this means God understands what we're going through; we can talk with him and know he's aware of what we're dealing with in life no matter where we are.

Preteen:

The onset of puberty isn't when you want someone watching you while you're naked—even if that someone is God. Let your preteen know that since God created him, he doesn't need to be embarrassed by what God sees. And knowing that God is completely aware of what we're doing offers a sense of security. Remind your preteen that, through Jesus, God has experienced what we're experiencing. God can relate—and because he knows every detail of our lives, God is someone with whom your preteen can talk. Because God is always there, always watching and listening, we can always turn to him.

Related Scriptures: Psalm 139; Matthew 10:30; and Hebrews 13:5 confirm that God knows us and is always with us.

How come God lets tornadoes and hurricanes hurt people?

Preschooler:
Reassure your preschooler that even though bad things sometimes happen, God always loves us. No matter what, he loves us. And when bad things happen, he is with us.

Elementary-Age:
Elementary-age children may wonder less about why God permits bad things and more about whether God is strong enough to *stop* them. Share with your child that God blesses both good people and bad people, and we're to accept both good and bad. And sometimes God allows hard things to happen for a reason we don't understand. We have to trust God, who has promised all things work for good (even bad things) for those who love him.

Preteen:
Help your preteen discover the world we live in *isn't* the world God designed. We live in an imperfect version of it, where bad things happen. Tornadoes, hurricanes, and other disasters are a consequence of sin entering the world through Adam and Eve. That sin had far-reaching consequences...just as our sin has far-reaching consequences, too. Read through the Scripture passages below together and search for an answer as to why God might let natural disasters exist. Be sure to check out Romans 8:28 as a reminder to trust God.

Related Scriptures: Numbers 16:30-34 and James 5:17 show God can control natural disasters; Romans 8:19-21 explains that sin has impacted nature as well as people.

Is Jesus really the only way to God?

Preschooler:
Explain Jesus came to help us know that God loves us, and to help us be friends with God. Your preschooler won't understand a comparison of world religions.

Elementary-Age:
Your child is being raised in a pluralistic society that values inclusiveness and tells us there are many ways to get close to God. Share that Jesus said he is the only way to God, and a friendship with Jesus is offered to everyone. He came for everyone; everyone is invited to benefit from his sacrifice on the cross.

Preteen:
Your preteen is exposed to a wide range of religions and beliefs about God. Share Jesus' claim that we all have a sin problem and he's the only solution to that problem, a bridge to God. His is an open invitation anyone can accept—it's not exclusionary. And that invitation also sets Christianity apart—no other religion tells of a God who offers love and forgiveness we don't have to earn. Your preteen might be concerned about being thought of as close-minded if she embraces biblical Christianity publicly, but that's a different issue: Jesus warned his followers they'd be in conflict with their cultures. That was true then—and it's true now. Ask your preteen what following Jesus will cost her socially…and if she's willing to pay the price.

Related Scriptures: Matthew 7:13-14; John 3:16; 14:6; and Romans 3:23 address Jesus' claim; see Matthew 10 regarding the cost of following Jesus.

If God wanted guys to be circumcised, why didn't he make them that way?

Preschooler:

It's unlikely your preschooler will ask this question. But should it come up, simply say it's something guys did in the Old Testament to mark themselves as people who love God. That answer will satisfy.

Elementary-Age:

Be ready to explain what circumcision is if asked: cutting extra skin off of a boy's penis. Explain circumcision was a sign of God's promise to love his people as they loved and followed him. Yes, it was painful. No, you don't know why God chose circumcision as a sign of his promise. Yes, God works in mysterious ways. And circumcision is something God wanted people to choose to do to show love for him.

Preteen:

Your preteen might find it perplexing that God chose to express his love through an act that brought pain to his male followers. Use the question as an opportunity to discuss how mysterious God is—and that we simply don't have all the answers. All we know is that it was a physical, visible way to show people's commitment to God—not something everyone did. Ask your preteen to think of modern ways people can show commitment to God.

Related Scriptures: Genesis 17:9-14 describes the covenant, and Isaiah 55:9 affirms that we don't always understand God's ways. Also see Philippians 3:1-3 and Colossians 2:8-12.

Q: God loves me...but does he like me?

Preschooler:

Hug your child as you describe God's love. Sing together "Jesus Loves Me," turning it into a two-verse song. Verse 1: "Jesus Loves Me." Verse 2: "Jesus *Likes* Me." And assure your child *you* like her.

Elementary-Age:

Reading the Related Scriptures below will be helpful, but always add hugs. If your child's question is motivated by guilt, ask if there's anything she needs to confess. Assure her God knows everything about her and still sent Jesus to rescue her. He's proven both his love and his acceptance for all his creations—including both of you! God doesn't always like what we do, but he always loves us, and he likes us because we're just the way he made us.

Preteen:

Preteens sometimes struggle with serious bouts of feeling unlikable— emotional storms that blow in quickly and with great severity. Assure your child God has proven his love through Jesus and—though he knows us intimately—still wants to spend eternity with us. Also, as you spend time with your child (maybe the best way to communicate you like him) share specific things you like about him. Share that the more time we spend with God, the more we'll see how much he likes us all the time, even if he doesn't like what we've done.

Related Scriptures: First John 3:1 tells us how we can see God's love even when the world doesn't love us. Psalm 139:14-16 talks about how carefully God made us just the way he wanted.

Q: I don't like church. Why do I have to go?

Preschooler:
Your preschooler is probably asking because he doesn't like being away from you or is bored or confused during church. Or there may be a child he doesn't like. Ask your child why he doesn't like church. If he doesn't want to be away from you, stay the course—separation anxiety can be overcome. If he's bored or confused or having trouble with another child, talk to your children's ministry leaders about your child's comments. You may also consider volunteering in your child's classroom. And let your child know church helps us grow closer to God and learn how to love him.

Elementary-Age:
Ask why church isn't a positive experience and talk about possible solutions. Consider getting involved and volunteering. Talk with your child's ministry leaders to seek insight about any conflicts. As a *last* resort, consider going to another church that provides a more satisfying program. In all this, make sure your child understands that church is important because we can build relationships with others who love Jesus.

Preteen:
When a preteen fails to connect with peers in church, it's likely the child will abandon church. Do whatever you can to involve your child in a healthy preteen ministry—even if it's not at your church. Help your child identify his gifts so he can invest them through the children's or preteen ministry at your church. Help your child understand church is a place to work together as people who love God and want to know him better.

Related Scriptures: Psalm 84:10 speaks to the joy, and Hebrews 10:25 to the mutual encouragement of being in church.

Am I going to hell since I did a bad thing?

Preschooler:
Tell your preschooler he should do good things, but not because he's afraid of hell. If he does something bad, he can tell you and God and be forgiven by you both. Let him know that Jesus loves him *always*—even when does something wrong.

Elementary-Age:
Explain that Jesus' forgiveness means we won't go to hell for doing bad things. God sent Jesus so we can all be in heaven with him. Remind your child he should always do the right thing, but that we all make mistakes. When we do something wrong, we can ask God to forgive us and apologize to those we've hurt.

Preteen:
Preteen children can understand that doing a bad thing is sin and we're all sinners. Your child's good or bad deeds won't determine if she goes to heaven or hell; what matters is that your child believes Jesus is her Savior. Confirm your child's choice to follow Jesus. And remind her that believing in Jesus isn't just about someday going to heaven—it's about spending now and forever with Jesus.

Related Scriptures: John 3:16 is a powerful verse about God's love and his desire for us. First John 1:9 talks about forgiveness.

How come the Bible is boring sometimes?

Preschooler:

Preschoolers aren't reading yet, so it's up to you to make Bible stories fun and exciting. Books and videos deliver content, but your enthusiasm will be contagious. Show you love the Bible and your preschooler will love it, too. Note: Group's *Pray & Play Bible* is a sturdy, preschooler-friendly Bible to place in the hands of your little one.

Elementary-Age:

Select an age-appropriate, easy-to-read version of the Bible—preferably one with explanations and activities. One option to consider: Group's *Hands-On Bible*. Determine why your child finds the Bible boring. Is it the content…style…perceived lack of relevance? Visit biblegateway.com with your child to find passages that relate to issues he's encountering. Relay that just like our own lives, some things in the Bible are more exciting than others. But if it's in the Bible, it's important to God.

Preteen:

Admit it…you find parts of the Bible boring, too. All those lists of names don't excite us, but they were all special people to God. Look on biblegateway.com for passages that relate to issues your child is facing, and read and discuss the passages together. Demonstrate by selecting an issue you're personally facing. Seeing Mom or Dad apply Bible truth is a powerful example.

Related Scriptures: Second Timothy 3:15-17 and Hebrews 4:12 speak to the authority and power of God's Word.

Q: **Does our church just want our money, like Dad says?**

Preschooler:
Explain that the money your family gives helps your pastor have a house. It also pays for the church building and all the things in it.

Elementary-Age:
Share that God doesn't actually *need* our money; God already owns everything. Explain that your giving lets you honor God and support ministries that are doing the work of God in your church, community, and around the world. Plus, your giving helps you be thankful for what you have. If your child receives income from you or elsewhere, encourage him to give a percentage to God's work in a disciplined way. Some elementary children find it especially meaningful to support another child through Compassion International or World Vision.

Preteen:
Preteens should not only be giving, but giving for the right reasons. Together with your child read the passages listed below. What is God saying about giving? Why might motives be more important than the amount of the gift? Focus on your child's heart, not his giving record. Consider securing a church budget to show your child costs for programming and missions.

Related Scriptures: Read and discuss Proverbs 19:17; Malachi 3:10-12; Matthew 6:1; 22:15-22; Mark 12:41-44; Luke 6:38; and 2 Corinthians 9:7.

Q: Why do angels watch us and let us still get into trouble?

Preschooler:

Your preschooler is learning to take responsibility for his actions. Tell him angels aren't like a policeman catching someone doing something wrong; they are there to help us as God tells them to. Most of the time, that doesn't include stopping us from doing bad things.

Elementary-Age:

Explain: Angels are God's messengers; they don't force us to make good decisions—though Psalm 91 makes a case that angels may provide protection. Let your child know there is someone who can help us make good choices: the Holy Spirit. Read the passages below about the Holy Spirit. Is your child allowing the Holy Spirit to work in his life? Together invite the Holy Spirit to work in you both.

Preteen:

Explain to your child there is a difference between angels and the Holy Spirit. Angels are God's messengers; the Holy Spirit helps us know right from wrong, if we're listening. Read the passages below about the Holy Spirit. Together, invite the Spirit to do his work in your child. Stress that we must take personal responsibility for our decisions, and that the consequences of decisions made during preteen years can be significant. Offer to be there for your child before, during, and after decisions he makes.

Related Scriptures: John 14:26 and Galatians 5:22-23 speak to the role of the Holy Spirit, and Philippians 2:12-13 and Matthew 25:31-46 the importance of our faith and actions. Also see Psalm 91.

Is Grandma an angel now that she died?

Preschooler:
Explain that angels aren't people who have gone to heaven, but if Grandma was friends with Jesus, she's in heaven with God and Jesus. And she'll be happy to see you all again.

Elementary-Age:
The simple answer is no, because angels are beings created by God, not Christians who've died and gone to heaven. Explore how your child feels about Grandma dying. Does she believe God "took" Grandma because he needed another angel? That common assurance, spoken to children, can create resentment toward God.

Preteen:
Again, the answer is no. Read the passages noted below. Assure your child that God cares for those who love him—even in death. If your preteen deeply misses her grandparent, be intentional about telling stories about Grandma and celebrating her life. Express your joy that one day you'll all be reunited in heaven.

Related Scriptures: Read 1 Peter 3:22; Psalm 148:2-5; Nehemiah 9:6; and Matthew 22:30 for insights into angels.

Q: How come God sends nice people to hell?

Preschooler:
Assure your preschooler that God's desire is for everyone to know him and love him and be with him forever. Tell your child that even nice people do bad things sometimes, and God won't be near those bad things because he's so perfect. But he'll forgive anyone who asks him to, because he doesn't want anyone to go to hell.

Elementary-Age:
Your elementary-age child is deciding what he believes...and a God who would let someone be tormented forever may not fit with the loving God who's been described in Sunday school. Stress that God is loving and just. Encourage your child to change his perspective. Going to hell is a consequence of our sins, because unforgiven sin can't be in God's presence—and even nice people have sinned. But God saves us from hell by forgiving us through Jesus. It's not God's desire that anyone should end up separated from him.

Preteen:
Jesus talked about hell and urged his followers to, through himself, assure themselves of eternity in heaven. Explore with your preteen how God has reached out to restore a relationship with his creation, most notably through Jesus, the Holy Spirit, and the Bible. Ask whether God chooses to separate himself from people or if it's their choice. Talk about God's grace in saving us from a punishment we all deserve, as sinners.

Related Scriptures: In Matthew 10:28 Jesus refers to hell; Romans 10:9-10 reminds us how to avoid hell.

Do people who kill themselves still go to heaven?

Preschooler:
Explain that we're very sad when people kill themselves, and God is sad, too. Admit that since God decides who goes to heaven because he knows what's in our heart, you don't really know. With your preschooler, pray for those who were left behind by a suicide; they're in pain.

Elementary-Age:
Ask what is motivating the question; it may be a signal your child or one of his friends is considering suicide. Share that suicide is often an impulsive, selfish act and doesn't give God the opportunity to bring healing into a situation. God decides who goes to heaven because he knows what's in our heart, and that includes people who've killed themselves. But he wants us to trust that he can help in a bad situation. If this question was prompted by a peer's suicide, find a capable grief counselor and be sure your child works through his emotions—now.

Preteen:
Again, determine if this is a signal that your child or a friend is considering suicide. Explore what might prompt a suicide attempt; listen carefully to determine if your child is experiencing any turmoil or hopelessness. Assure your child that people who have chosen to believe in Jesus will go to heaven even if they kill themselves, but God desires that they trust him to take care of their problems. If you suspect your child is considering suicide, seek professional help immediately.

Related Scriptures: Our bodies aren't our own; see 1 Corinthians 6:19. And Exodus 20:13 commands us to not murder—anyone. That includes ourselves.

Q: What's heaven really like?

Preschooler:

This question may arise after a death or be prompted by curiosity or a growing knowledge of Jesus. Preschoolers think concretely and have a hard time picturing something they can't see. Share that heaven is a place where we'll be with God forever and never be sad again.

Elementary-Age:

John's description of heaven as a city of precious jewels, pearl gates, and golden streets may help, or it may sound boring to your child. Tell your child heaven is a perfect place where we'll never be sad and nothing bad will happen. That still doesn't answer practical questions: *What will we eat? Where will we sleep?* Assure your child that even though we don't know the answers to those questions, we do know heaven is better than they can imagine and God will take care of everything.

Preteen:

Your preteen may be concerned about getting into heaven, so reassure her that if she's given her life to Jesus, she'll be in heaven. Stress that Jesus didn't provide many details about heaven, simply promising he would prepare a place there for his followers. Although we don't know exactly what it's like, we know it's better than the best thing we can imagine and that we'll never be sad there. Ask your preteen if she trusts Jesus to take care of her; that's the key issue.

Related Scriptures: Revelation 21:18-21 gives a physical description of heaven. Also see John 14:1-6.

How come I can't visit heaven first to see if I like it?

Preschooler:
Your preschooler might be concerned about being separated from you, or be afraid of being sent somewhere she won't like. Tell your child heaven isn't a place we can go visit because it's a special place for after this life. Assure your child Jesus is preparing heaven to be a special, fun place where your child can be with Jesus—and you!—forever.

Elementary-Age:
Explain that heaven is reserved for *after* we finish life on earth and that Jesus has arranged a wonderful place for us that we can only imagine until we actually get there (since we can't get there on an airplane now). Ask why your child is uncertain about wanting to be in heaven. What's behind the question? Together, read the Scriptures listed below and ask your child if he's willing to trust Jesus to take care of arrangements in heaven.

Preteen:
Your preteen is old enough to understand that while heaven is very real, it isn't a physical place we can point to on a map. We can't get there in a plane or car. But we can trust that we'll like it, because Jesus said he's preparing it as a place just for us.

Related Scriptures: You can trust God—see Luke 12:32 and John 14:3.

Q: Do pets go to heaven?

Preschooler:
Reassure preschoolers who are curious, or grieving the loss of a pet, that God cares about his creations—including pets. While the Bible doesn't address this question specifically, you can comfortably say that God cares about our pets.

Elementary-Age:
Losing a pet for children this age can be painful, even if there didn't seem to be a strong relationship between the child and pet. While we're not sure about pets and heaven, help your child to know God is sad when we're sad. He also promises to care for all creatures. Having a small ceremony with prayer for the dead pet helps bring closure.

Preteen:
Explain the only way for people to go to heaven is by having a personal friendship with Jesus. Although animals can't decide to believe in Jesus, God cares deeply about what we care about and love. We don't know if pets will go to heaven, but we're certain God has a plan for our eternal life and we can trust God with our lives...and our pets.

Related Scriptures: Psalm 145:9 helps younger children understand God's love for all creatures. Some older children may find Romans 8:18-25 helpful.

Q: Will I go to hell for my bad thoughts?

Preschooler:
Your preschooler is more likely to ask the question like this: What happens if I think bad things? Explain that our thoughts matter—they can help us be happy or sad, feel safe or scared. God forgives us for thinking about bad things if we ask. Pray with your child for God's forgiveness.

Elementary-Age:
Help your child connect the dots: What we think about impacts what we do. If we stop misbehavior at the "thought" step, we have fewer consequences than if we act. Ask your child why he thinks his thoughts are "hell-worthy." Assure him of God's grace—and the Holy Spirit's willingness to lead him closer to God. Make sure your child knows that Jesus can forgive any sinful thought or action, so we don't need to worry about anything sending us to hell if we have a relationship with him.

Preteen:
The quick answer is no: A relationship with Jesus means we're forgiven for anything and we won't go to hell. But if your child can't control his fantasies, suggest he control what he allows to fuel his thoughts. What media does he consume? Is it healthy, or not? A caution: A quick read of Matthew 5:27-28 suggests that if you think something it's as bad as if you do it. Not so. Jesus was saying the thought and action come from the same root—and one can easily lead to the other. Read Philippians 4:8 and encourage your child to replace bad thoughts with good ones.

Related Scriptures: God seeks to renew our thoughts—see Romans 12:1-2; 2 Corinthians 10:5; Philippians 4:8; and 1 John 1:9. And thoughts lead to actions: See Matthew 5:28.

Imponderables

Q: I hate school. Why do I have to go?

Preschooler:
Listen first, fix second. Why does your child hate preschool? It may be separation anxiety or an ongoing conflict. It may be embarrassment about a potty-training incident. Understand and then address the core issue. Let your child know school is an important part of learning things he'll need to know as he grows up.

Elementary-Age:
Listen for the core reasons your child dislikes school. Be clear: No elementary-school dropouts at your house. School teaches important things all kids need to know. But be equally clear: God doesn't let us walk through hard places alone. He'll help—and so will you. Honor your child's issues, and brainstorm and pray together how to tackle the core issues behind his dislike of school.

Preteen:
Tell your child that mastering school is his job right now; it's how he can prepare for his future. And by working hard at it, he can show love for God. Attending school isn't punishment—it's preparation. Share that disliking or struggling with current classes doesn't mean school will always be distasteful. If your getting involved at the school will help, gain your child's approval to take that step. Pray together because God "gets it"…even Jesus likely had to go to synagogue school.

Related Scriptures: Luke 2:40 and Colossians 3:23 tells us how to approach school. Proverbs 1:7 reveals the source of true wisdom.

Why is it a bad thing to put my middle finger up in the air?

Preschooler:

No need for details! Simply explain your preschooler's middle fingers aren't bad fingers, and gently tell your child to avoid lifting it toward others because it's rude. And ask who encouraged your preschooler to do it—that may prompt *another* conversation.

Elementary-Age:

Your child may not fully understand that "flipping the bird" is a visual shortcut meaning an obscene act, likely to result in someone taking great offense. Be clear about what the gesture means: It's a way of saying something rude to put a person down. If the question was prompted by receiving the gesture, encourage forgiveness. If you're having the conversation because your child inflicted it on others, help your child practice an apology, and encourage her to follow through.

Preteen:

Unless your preteen lives in a cave, he's seen this gesture…and maybe flashed it at others. Encourage your child to *not* reflect the rudeness and obscenity of the culture, but to deal with his anger in more positive ways—ways that can lead to reconciliation. Your child can calmly and clearly express feelings by saying, "That makes me feel angry because…" and that's more likely to result in a resolution to a problem.

Related Scriptures: See Matthew 5:43-48 and Romans 14:13. Does flipping the bird draw anyone closer to Jesus…or push them further away?

Is it okay to kill people if you're a soldier?

Preschooler:

Preschoolers are too young to comprehend war. If your preschooler has a connection with the military, the question behind this might be: *Is Daddy or Mommy doing bad things?* Assure your child that soldiers aren't bad people.

Elementary-Age:

In the Old Testament, God blessed war in certain circumstances. Yet one of the Ten Commandments is to not kill. What gives? There are sincere Christians who are pacifists...deployed soldiers in combat zones...and all points in between. Tell your child that Christians believe different things about war, and engage your child in meaningful conversation about what he thinks. The Scripture passages below will help you frame your discussion.

Preteen:

Offer your opinion but acknowledge this is a tough question that has divided the church. Talk about your struggles, if any, with this topic. Encourage your child to draw his own conclusions—prayerfully.

Related Scriptures: See Exodus 20:13; also see Joshua 4:13 and 1 Samuel 15:3.

If God says not to kill, why do we eat animals?

Preschooler:
Explain that when God said to not kill, he meant to not kill another person. It's okay to eat a hamburger, because God gave people plants and animals as food. But God never wants us to kill another person, because people are special.

Elementary-Age:
Explain the difference between killing a person and an animal—the answer above and Scripture references below will be helpful. Explore if your child is feeling guilty about killing animals for food and might want to embrace vegetarianism or other dietary alternatives. If so, explore it—but be sure your child doesn't do so because of a misunderstanding of what God said about killing.

Preteen:
Again, the basic principles are the same. But your preteen may have additional reasons for asking about killing animals. Gently probe to discover if your preteen wonders if animals have souls…or whether vegetarianism is a more spiritually aware lifestyle. Exploring why your preteen is asking this might lead to other, more important conversations.

Related Scriptures: See Genesis 9:1-7. And in Mark 14:12-18, Jesus eats lamb.

Why do I have to be nice to people I don't like?

Preschooler:
Tell your preschooler about the Golden Rule—being nice to others just like we want them to be nice to us. Suggest specific situations and rehearse what applying the Golden Rule might look like in your preschooler's life. Model it at home and point out when you're showing it in action.

Elementary-Age:
Your elementary-age child can grasp the concept of altruistic kindness: giving with no immediate reward. Help your child apply that concept to people he actively dislikes—because doing so pleases God and shows that your child loves God and others. Share stories from your life about when you've been kind to those who were unkind to you. How did you feel? What did it change in your life?

Preteen:
Your preteen's world can be brutal. Competition, back-biting, unfair comparisons…it's easy for preteens to develop a callous attitude toward others simply as a defensive mechanism. Encourage your preteen to consider why someone might be acting mean, and coach your child to see beyond just the surface. Encourage your child that showing kindness to enemies may help them understand Jesus better.

Related Scriptures: Jesus tells us to pray for bullies (and others) in Matthew 5:44. See also Matthew 22:37-40.

How come some people hurt themselves on purpose?

Preschooler:
The psychology of self-injury is beyond your preschooler's comprehension, but your child does understand that people get sick. Explain that self-injury is an illness and those who suffer need the help of doctors.

Elementary-Age:
It's likely if you're elementary student is asking, she's encountered a specific situation among her peers. Cutting and other self-mutilation sometimes occurs among older elementary-age children. Be sure your child understands this is an illness—not a fad to be emulated or a way to draw attention and sympathy.

Preteen:
Your child is ready for a fuller explanation of self-mutilation. Explain that physical pain can momentarily distract people from emotional pain. Ask your child if she's seen evidence of cutting, scarring, or other self-mutilation among peers. Stress that even if an incident appears to be staged for drama, it's a dangerous dip into dark behavior and the help of an adult professional is needed immediately.

Related Scriptures: See 1 Peter 5:7; Leviticus 19:28; and 1 Corinthians 6:20—they reflect God's attitude toward the gift of our bodies.

Q: **If I'm supposed to be nice to people in wheelchairs, why do you tell me not to stare at them?**

Preschooler:

Let your preschooler know it's considered rude to stare at people and that the feelings of those in wheelchairs may be hurt if we stare. Most children this age can relate to hurt feelings. Advise preschoolers to smile and even say "hi!" instead of staring.

Elementary-Age:

Remind your child that God created and loves everyone, and we need to treat everyone with kindness and respect. The Bible tells us to treat others as we would like to be treated. We sometimes stare at people who are different from us because we're curious. Tell your child it's okay to be curious about how and why people are different, and encourage your child to ask you any questions about disabilities. Unsure about the details of a disability? Do a web search for information together.

Preteen:

Yes, we should be nice to everyone…but we sometimes aren't certain how that looks. Challenge your preteens to live out their faith by interacting with the disabled rather than watching from afar.

Related Scriptures: Luke 6:31 is a good reminder of the Golden Rule. Mark 2:1-12 shows us how friends cared for their disabled friend.

Q: Why do people get divorced?

Preschooler:
Preschoolers won't fully comprehend the concept of divorce. Explain that sometimes people decide to not stay married or live in the same house anymore. If your preschooler probes further, tell him people divorce because they're not happy together. If you're talking about your own divorce, reassure your preschooler that both his parents love him and your divorce isn't his fault. Clarify how your divorce will affect his living situation.

Elementary-Age:
Elementary-age children understand some married people don't get along and divorce. If your child brings up divorce because of what he heard about someone else, reassure him you're happy and he doesn't need to worry. However, if you're going through a divorce, encourage him to talk about his feelings. Hug often—reassure him he's not at fault and that you both love him!

Preteen:
Preteens understand divorce although they're less willing to accept it. You can tell your preteen that sometimes married people decide they don't love each other any more, but she's more likely to ask about your family's specific situation. Be honest—but don't go into every detail. Don't assign blame. Explain that while God doesn't like divorce, he knows divorces happen and he still loves everyone.

Related Scriptures: Malachi 2:16 and Matthew 19:1-12 can guide your discussion with older children.

Q: Does the Bible say people can't get married twice?

Preschooler:
Preschoolers want concrete answers. So simply put, the Bible does *not* say people can't get married twice. However, clarify that people can only be married to one person at a given time.

Elementary-Age:
Inform your child the Bible allows remarriage under certain circumstances, such as when widowed. Using the passages below, explain what the Bible says about divorce and remarriage: God values marriage, and in most cases God doesn't want divorced people to marry again. You can share how God provided a new husband for Ruth after her first husband died.

Preteen:
No, the Bible doesn't say that people can't get married twice in certain circumstances. God loves people and wants them to obey him, and part of that is following his plan for marriage. There are Bible verses that describe when people can get married again, but the bigger message is that God wants to teach us to love and obey him—and value marriage.

Related Scriptures: Matthew 5:32; and Matthew 19:9 speak to God's feelings about divorce. The book of Ruth is an example of a woman who loved God and who also remarried.

How come some people have to be pushed around in wheelchairs?

Preschooler:
It's hard to understand suffering. Tell your child that some people's legs don't work, but when we're in heaven with God, we'll all be healthy and happy.

Elementary-Age:
Elementary-age children wonder how God can let people hurt if he loves them. Help your child see that great good can come out of suffering. A person who's hurt may rely on God more, become a great artist since he can't run, or encourage another who is in a wheelchair. Have your child think about when she was sick or hurt and how she encouraged someone with the same experience.

Preteen:
Preteens can understand God never wanted suffering...that it's a result of sin in the world. A difficult part of faith is trusting God even when we don't understand what's happening or think God should do something different. God can use suffering to bring us closer to him, encourage others, help us be thankful, grow our relationship with Christ, and even bring people to Jesus.

Related Scriptures: Romans 8:28 says God uses all for good, and Proverbs 3:5 reminds us to trust God.

Is Santa Claus real? What about the Easter Bunny?

Preschooler:
Some people avoid imaginary characters like Santa and the Easter Bunny while others embrace them. Regardless of your preference, the focus of Christmas and Easter is the birth and resurrection of Christ. If your child asks a direct question, tell the truth: They're pretend ways to bring love and joy. Even if your child is upset or angry, or you feel that you're spoiling the fun, your long-term credibility is more important than your child's short-term sadness.

Elementary-Age:
Children who've experienced Santa and the Bunny will begin questioning practical matters like fitting down chimneys. Friends will share the truth, so do so yourself. Let your child know that the idea of Santa Claus is based on a real man, Saint Nicholas, who gave presents to people in his village. Most children will say, "I knew Santa wasn't real!" while others may be disappointed. Caution your children to let others find out the truth themselves.

Preteen:
Most preteens don't believe, but they may enjoy playing along and helping—especially with younger siblings. Playing Santa or the Easter Bunny is an opportunity to show Jesus' love. Encourage your preteen to think of ways to keep Jesus the focus of these holidays. You may also help your preteen research the history of Santa and the Easter Bunny, and talk about how these characters were rooted in showing love.

Related Scriptures: Matthew 1:18-25 tells about the birth of Jesus. Deuteronomy 6:6-9 addresses your responsibility for training and truth.